# FIFTY Handprints

## A Practical Guide to Knowledge of Scientific Palmistry

**(Predictions and Remedies Included)**

**Prof. Dayanand and Nisha Ghai**
**Scientific Palmists**



**D K's Books For All**
(an imprint of Low Price Publications)
**Delhi**

Published by
**D K's Books For All**
(an imprint of Low Price Publications)
A-6, Nimri Commercial Centre,
Near Ashok Vihar Phase-IV,
Delhi-110052
Phones: 27302453
e-mail: lpp@nde.vsnl.net.in
visit us at: www.lppindia.com



First Published 2006

ISBN 81-7386-272-9

Printed at
**D K Fine Art Press P Ltd.**
Delhi-110052



PRINTED IN INDIA

## *Contents*

## *Foreword*

# A Journey from Secretive Knowledge to Scientific Palmistry

I was 17-years old at that time. During those days I had read a book on palmistry that forecasted the future. I too, by studying the palms of my friends and relatives, began to predict their future, when asked.

It was mentioned in the book that one who has a long Line of Saturn is rich. A person with a short Line of Life has a short life. A long Line of Life bisected by the Line of Mercury proves dangerous for his life. If the lines of marriage are more than one, then the person has more than one marriage or many love affairs. The vertical lines present on the lines of marriage indicate the number of children born to the person.

On the basis of knowledge acquired from that book, when I studied the hands of my acquaintances, I began to doubt the validity of this knowledge. This was because many of my close friends had no Line of Saturn but were rich, while I saw a long Line of Saturn on the hands of many of my acquaintances living in poverty. I came across the hands of a number of persons according to whose Line of Life, they should have died at the age of 50, but who were hail and hearty, right in front of me, even at the age of 65.

To remove my doubts, I read many other books related to palmistry but they only helped to add to my state of confusion. In some books the start of the Line of Heart was mentioned as the base of the index finger; while in others, the emergence of the Line of Heart was given at the base of the little or the fourth finger.

I found different views regarding the Line of Mercury. In some books, it was described as the Line of Health while in others, it had been named as 'hepatica'.

One other line—the Girdle of Venus—kept me in a state of dilemma for a long time. This is because the Mount of Venus is at the base of the thumb and the Girdle of Venus is said to lie below the ring finger and the middle finger. The result of having such a line is that the person with this girdle has excess of sexual desires. But in my practical experience, I discovered the Girdle of Venus on the palms of many of my close acquaintances but I did not see any signs of excessive sexual desire in them.

There was also a variation in the names of the lines and the interpretations made in European and American books on palmistry in comparison to India's *Samudrika Shastra.*

In order to get to the root of the reality, I expressed my dilemma to an author of many books on palmistry. He replied, "This is a secret knowledge. To acquire knowledge in this field, you need to possess the inner eye." I was however not satisfied with his reply.

Many institutions were there to teach how to make future predictions through horoscopes; however, knowledge about palmistry had to be obtained only through books written decades ago.

On seeing this situation, I resolved to study deeply this so-called secretive knowledge; and the knowledge that I acquired, I decided to disseminate among others.

As time passed, my interest in knowledge about palmistry turned towards psychology too. On reaching middle age, my interest reached the stage of spiritualism. By studying disciplines like palmistry, psychology and spirituality, I reached the conclusion that our life is like a continuously flowing stream. The flow of this stream continues from the past to the future births.

Modern science does not believe in either previous life or future rebirths, but accepts the presence of genes. It has been proved by science that we receive these genes from our ancestors and these we pass on to our children.

There is one similarity between the knowledge of spiritualism and the science of genetics—that is, before this birth, we had a distinct identity and after our death, this identity would continue to stay in some form or other. In ancient Hindu texts, this has been referred to as the soul or sanskar (instincts of previous birth). Modern science gives it names like genes, instinct, unconscious mind, subconscious, etc.

I passed 60 years of my life in trying to trace the missing links between books on palmistry, psychology and knowledge of spiritualism. During this period, I studied thousands of palms among which were the hands of different members of a particular family, including the handprints of one particular person taken after a gap of several years.

On a careful study of the Indian treatise, *Samudrika Shastra* and the books on palmistry written by European and American authors and those of other countries coupled with my experience gained after studying various hands for 40 years, I established the Institute of Palmistry in 1989. The objective of the Institute is to propagate and spread information on the scientific aspects of palmistry.

Here I wish to clarify that by use of the word 'scientific', I do not mean that it is a science like physics, chemistry, etc.; what I mean is that it is psychology.

In establishment of the Institute I received the cooperation of my daughter Nisha Ghai. She has assisted me in imparting education through the Institute as also in propagating this knowledge through the medium of the Internet among various foreign countries; further, at the time of hand reading, she has helped me as I could discuss and exchange views with her on palmistry.

I cannot claim that I have unearthed all the layers of this knowledge that have been considered secretive; all I wish to say is that I have embarked on the path of search for this knowledge. Life is short; the journey through life is long. What all I have learnt, I am disseminating that among others. I have hopes that after me, my daughter Nisha Ghai will complete whatever I would have left unfinished.

In the first chapter of this book, a brief note on the research activities of the Institute are given. Description of this research is given in the books published by the Institute. Hence, a brief description is being provided about them for the benefit of those curious readers, who have not read these books and who wish to learn the basis for the predictions made by the Institute.

In the second chapter, handprints and remedies of 38 persons caught in different kinds of problems have been given.

In the third chapter, handprints are given of different members of one particular family or of one particular person during different age groups in his life. In this manner inquisitive persons can get the opportunity to carry out a comparative study.

In the fourth chapter, those descriptions and remedies to overcome obstacles have been provided which have been referred to in the second and third chapters.

It is hoped that this book can prove helpful to those who are keen to acquire practical knowledge of palmistry.

**Dayanand**

## *Chapter 1*

# Basis for Future Predictions According to Research Undertaken by the Institute of Palmistry

The handprints given in this book have been selected from the handprints taken of thousands of people who visit the Institute. To provide answers to questions raised by the clients regarding their future, we made the findings of this Institute the basis for our study.

The findings of our research on palmistry have been published in the form of books given below:

- Palmistry Guide
- All the Secrets of Palmistry
- Palmistry, How to Master It
- A Hand Book of Scientific and Practical Palmistry

Here I feel it would be essential to give a brief synopsis on these books for the benefit of knowledge-seekers who have not read these books, so that they can derive full advantage from this present book.

According to our hypothesis, the mounts on the palm are magnetic centres and the lines on the palm are the paths for electric currents that are produced by the brain. The magnetic centres of the palm attract these electrical currents towards themselves. These currents travelling through the nerves to the interior of the body remain invisible till they reach the wrist. As soon as they cross the wrist, paths of currents appear on the palm. These paths are known as 'palm lines' in everyday language.

A description of this hypothesis has been published in our book "A Hand Book of Scientific and Practical Palmistry" hence, instead of expounding on this subject, we wish to introduce human nature on the basis of the mounts and the fingers. This is because the nature of a man has a major role to play in making or marring his future.

**Mounts and Fingers of the Palm**

The mount at the base of the index finger (the first finger) that is next to the thumb is called the Mount of Jupiter (see Figure 1). This mount indicates the strength of man's ego and the magnitude of his desire to gain recognition and fame. The index finger is representative of the qualities of the Mount of Jupiter.

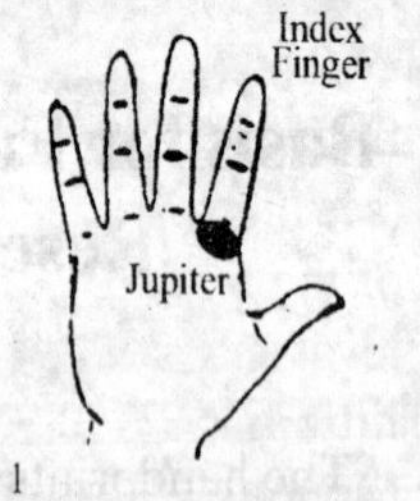

Fig. 1

The area at the base of the middle finger (the central finger) that lies next to the index finger is called the Mount of Saturn. This mount (see Figure 2) indicates the temperament of the person, his desire for solitude, his introvert nature, and the strength of his analytical power. Normally this mount is depressed, so the characteristics of this mount are judged by the length of the middle finger.

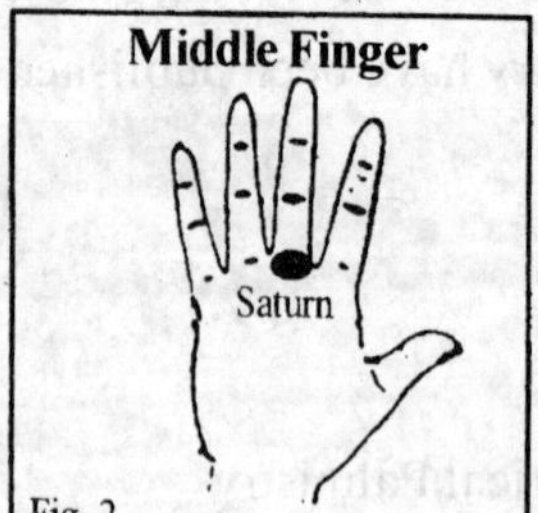

Fig. 2

The middle finger is longer than all the other fingers of the hand. A person with a longer-than-normal middle finger has greater characteristics of the Mount of Saturn.

The third or the ring finger, which lies next to the middle finger, indicates the tendency towards being extrovert, rash or prone to take hasty decisions. The portion of the palm at the base of the ring finger is called the Mount of Sun or Apollo. Figure 3 shows vertical lines on the Mount of Sun indicating success and fame. Horizontal lines on the Mount of Sun indicate obstacles in one's path. This mount is normally

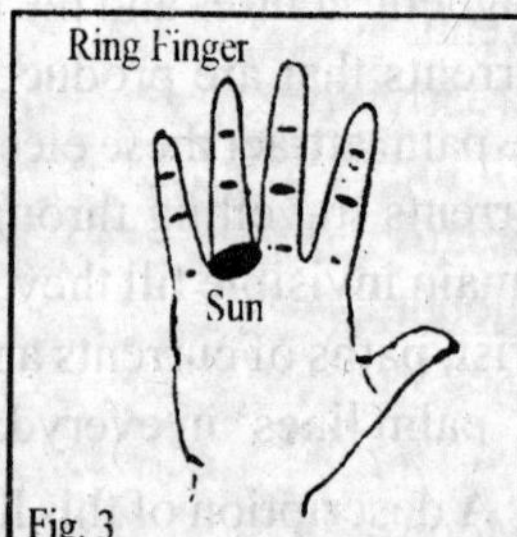

Fig. 3

depressed. Vertical lines on this mount indicate the results of its development. One or two vertical lines are auspicious; but too many vertical lines signify hurdles in his success.

The fourth finger next to the ring finger is the little finger that is indicative of the man's practical approach, his eloquence and the degree of sexual desire.

The portion of the palm below this finger is known as the Mount of Mercury (see Figure 4). You will find that the setting of the little finger is normally at a lower level on the palm. A thick and high-placed little finger is equivalent to a developed Mount of Mercury.

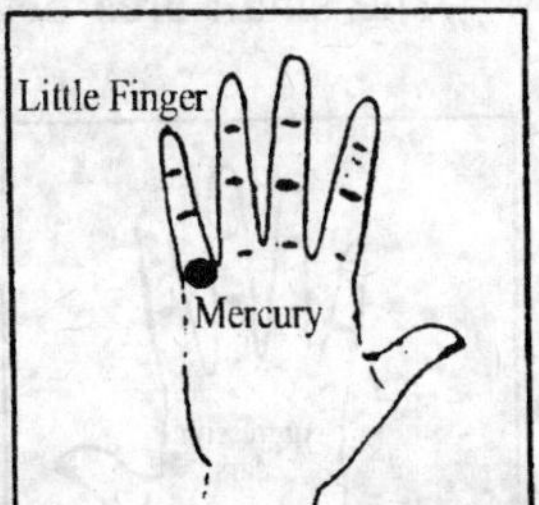

Fig. 4

The portion below the thumb and up to the wrist is called the Mount of Venus (see Figure 5). This mount reveals the capacity of man and woman to maintain their relations on a favourable ground, besides indicating the man's capacity to give birth to progeny and the power of his sexuality. His mount depicts the relations between his parents, his siblings and between him and his wife.

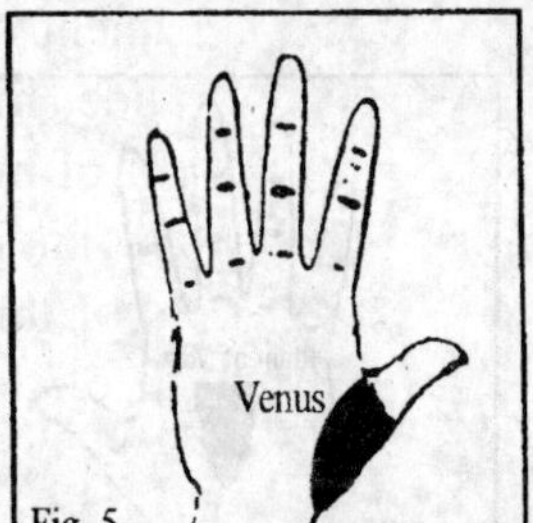

Fig. 5

The thumb reveals the characteristics of a man's mind. A short thick thumb signifies a limited growth of his mind while a thin, long thumb conveys an extra development of the mind.

The portion in front of the Mount of Venus till the wrist tells about the person's creative ability and desire for travel or change of residence. Journeys and creativity are indicated by the lines on this mount, which is called the Mount of Moon (see Figure 6).

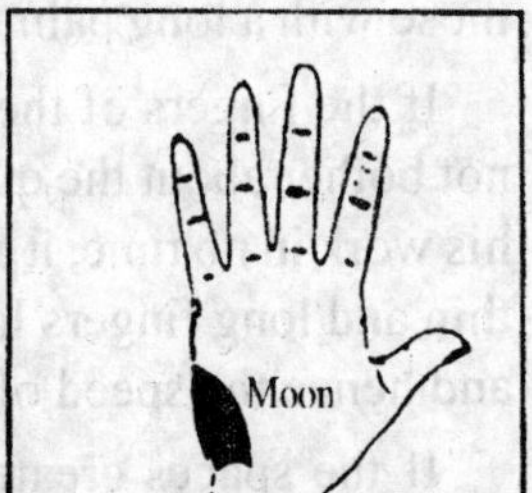

Fig. 6

The small part between the Mount of Moon and the Mount of Mercury conveys the amount of patience and tolerance the person has (see Figure 7). In ancient books of palmistry, this mount has been called the Upper Mars. The books published by the Institute have named this mount as the Defensive Mars as per its characteristics.

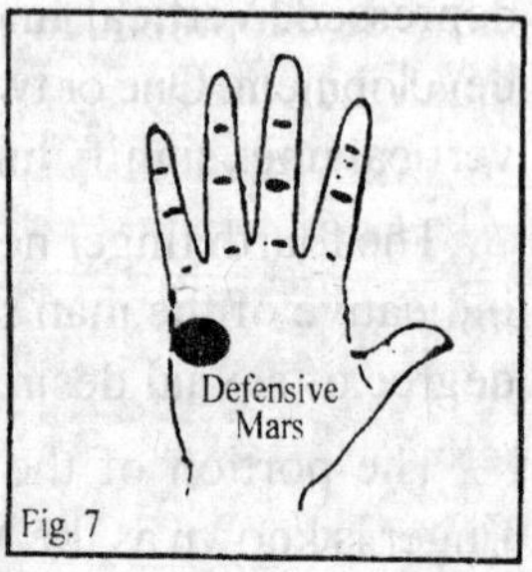

Fig. 7

The small area between the Mount of Venus and the Mount of Jupiter indicates the aggressive nature or the tendency to dominate (see Figure 8). In ancient books of palmistry, this mount has been called Lower Mars. According the books published by the Institute, this mount has been referred to as Aggressive Mars.

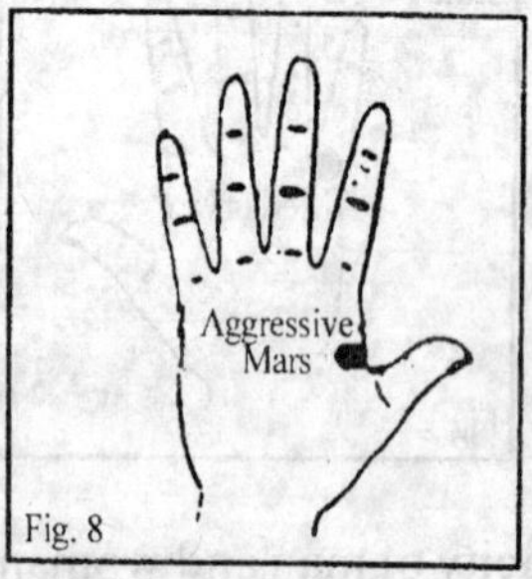

Fig. 8

The area of the palm between all these mounts tells us about the extent of courage seen in a person. This mount is called the Plain of Mars (see Figure 9).

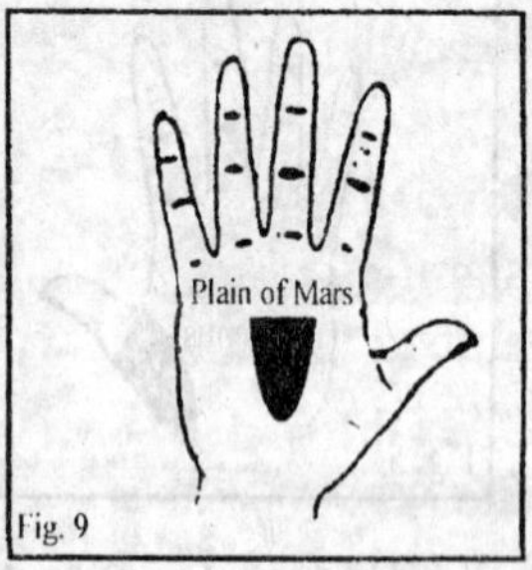

Fig. 9

## Other Features of the Palm and the Fingers

Persons with a thick and heavy hand do not lose courage easily, while those with narrow and thin hands tend to give up easily.

A person with a broad palm has greater strength to do work; those with a long palm are usually adept at planning.

If the fingers of the hand are small and thick, the person does not bother about the quality of the work he does. As he completes his work in no time, it affects the quality of his work. Persons with thin and long fingers love to go into the minor details of the work and hence the speed of their execution of work is slow.

If the spaces created between the fingers on spreading them out are equal, then the characteristics of the mounts of the fingers show development in a balanced manner. If the spaces are not equal, then the person's inability to deal with others is indicated.

As an example, if the distance between the index and the middle fingers is more, then the person is very keen to find acceptance and respect. If the space between the little and the ring fingers is more, then the person loves to exercise his own wishes. The space between the two middle fingers is normally less. If the space is more, then the person tries to escape from his responsibilities.

## A Brief Overview of Our Experiences Regarding the Lines on the Palm

### *Line of Life (see Figure 10)*

This line is found on all hands. The Line of Life that moves in a circular manner to reach the wrist indicates a sound physical position. A Line of Life with islands (see Figure 10A) indicates poor health as also a poor financial situation. A person with a straight Line of Life has to lead a life of struggle in the initial period of his life.

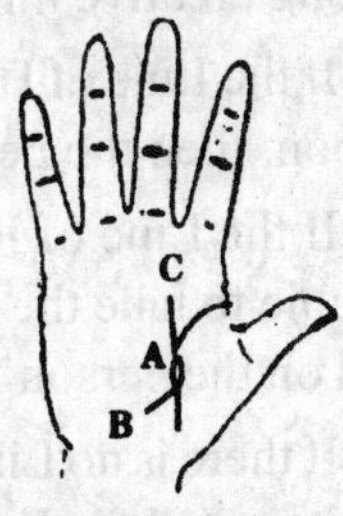

Fig. 10

If a branch of the Line of Life moves towards the Mount of Moon, then it signifies the person's tendency to travel abroad (see Figure 10B).

If the Line of Life finishes towards the Mount of Moon, then the person settles abroad.

If a branch of the Line of Life moves towards the fingers, then it points to fulfilment of the person's desires (see Figure 10C). Every person has a different desire. One may want fame, the other may desire wealth, and yet another may seek a child, a marriage, a divorce, expansion of business or an employment. Whatever be the person's desire, this branch conveys the fulfilment of that desire.

A short Line of Life indicates family problems after middle age.

### *Line of Head (see Figure 11)*

The Line of Head conveys the quality of the brain. Answers on questions related to wealth depend on the quality of the auspiciousness or inauspiciousness of the line. This line rises close to the beginning of the Line of Life and ends towards the Defensive Mars (see Figure 11A).

If there is space at the beginning of the Line of Head and the Line of Life, then the person gives prime importance to his own desires.

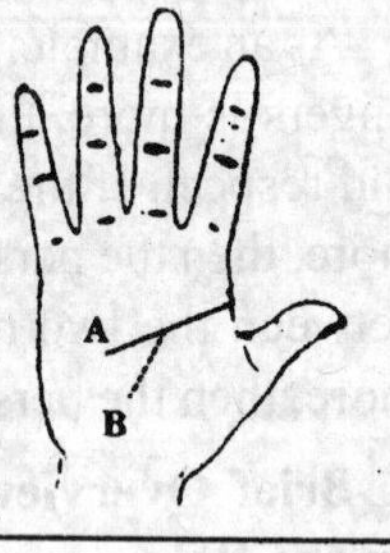

Fig. 11

If the Line of Head and Line of Life are close together for a long distance, then the person's initial life is led according to the wishes of his family. If the Line of Head rises inside the Line of Life or from the Aggressive Mars, then the person is short-tempered.

If the direction of the Line of Head is towards the Mount of Moon or the Luna Mount (see Figure 11B), then the person has a strong creative mind.

If the Line of Head is inclined completely towards the Mount of Moon, then the person remains lost in a world of dreams.

If the Line of Head is broken or is full of islands, the person is unable to take the right decision at the right moment. Its ill effects fall on the person's destiny too.

If there is no Line of Head on the hand, but only the Line of Heart is present, then the person's decisions are essentially emotional.

The reason for his ill lick is his inability to deal properly with others and due to his being extra sensitive. If there is only the Line of Head and there is no Line of Heart, then the person lacks emotions and has the tendency to be self-centred and selfish.

***Line of Heart (see Figure 12)***

The spot from which the Line of Heart rises is either below the Mount of Jupiter or the Mount of Saturn, and it ends at the base of the Mount of Mercury. A much too long a Line of Heart is indicative of an extra emotional nature. Those with an excessively short Line of Heart do not fall prey to emotions but are more practical and work according the benefits that they will gain.

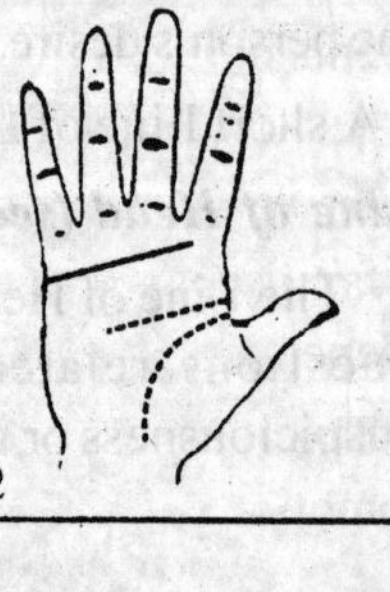
Fig. 12

A broken Line of Heart in the form of a chain is indicative of problems in love, affection, friendship and other such relationships.

If the Line of Heart lies close to the base of the fingers, then the person is more emotional in his feelings towards others. If the Line of Heart is farther from the base of the fingers but is close to the Line of Head, then such a person is good in personal dealings with others.

If the branches of the Line of Heart and the Line of Head bisect each other, then the person shows no balance in decision-making. Thus, this has an ill effect on his destiny.

***Line of Saturn (see Figure 13)***

Palmists in the olden era used to call this line as the Line of Fate. This line informs about the efforts made towards acquiring wealth, treasure, employment, marriage, partnership and other such issues. This line normally rises close to the wrist (see Figure 13A) or at the Mount of Moon (see Figure 13B) or within the Line of Life (see Figure 13C) or it can be in the form a branch of the Line of Life (see Figure 13D). No matter from where it rises, if its direction is towards the Mount of Saturn, then it will inevitably be called the Line of Saturn.

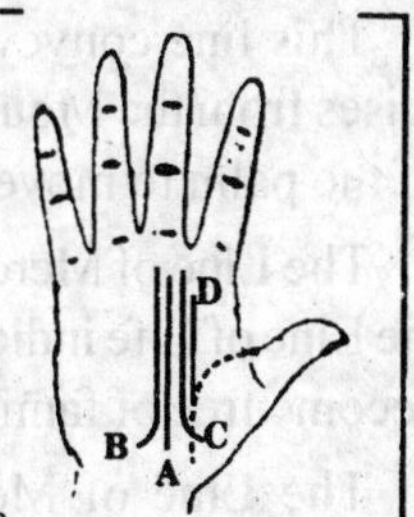

Fig. 13

The Line of Saturn that rises on the Mount of Moon indicates the advantages that will accrue from acquaintances who are not relations from either the maternal or paternal side of the family. Lines that cut across the Line of Saturn after emerging from the Mount of Moon or Defensive Mars are indicative of the obstacles placed or harm caused by outsiders. Lines that emerge from the Line of Life to bisect the Line of Saturn indicate the obstacles raised by relatives of a person's parents or members of the paternal family.

The Line of Saturn emerging from the Line of Life indicates that the person's youth is dependent upon the wishes of his parents or family. After crossing the Line of Life, the person becomes independent and self-sufficient.

The Line of Saturn informs about the efforts put in to acquire promotion, wealth, employment, etc. The success of these efforts is gauged from the position of the supportive line to this Line of Saturn.

***Line of Sun (see Figure 14A)***

This is the main supportive line of the Line of Saturn. This line emerges from the wrist to run through the centre of the palm, i.e. the Mount of Moon, before moving in the direction of the Mount of Sun.

The age at which the Line of Sun arises, then efforts made from that age according to the Line of Saturn will bear fruits of success. These efforts pertain to employment, marriage, love, divorce, wealth, house/property, foreign travel or any other field.

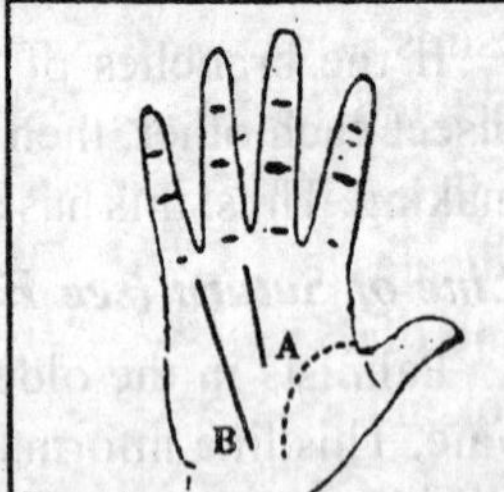

Fig. 14

***Line of Mercury (see Figure 14B)***

This line conveys the practical knowledge of a man. The line arises from the Mount of Venus or the Mount of Moon or the centre of the palm to move in the direction of the Mount of Mercury.

The Line of Mercury that rises from the Mount of Venus to cross the Line of Life indicates that the person after crossing his youth will become free of family responsibilities and achieve success.

The Line of Mercury emanating from the Mount of Moon indicates success in efforts related to travel. A clear Line of Mercury indicates the person's power of understanding. A broken line or a line with islands indicates poor health and the harm caused due to wrong decisions taken in life.

***Line/Lines of Sexuality (Figure 15)***

Emanating at the base of the little finger and coming from outside the palm, the small line/lines convey information about sexual relations of the person. Divorce, love, spouse's health or information about marital problems is received from these lines. But to obtain a clear answer to these questions, it is essential to look at the auspicious/ inauspicious aspects of the Line of Saturn and its supportive lines.

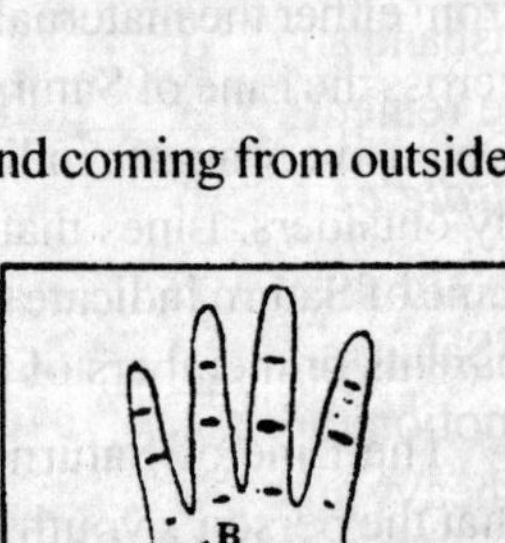

Fig. 15

The Line of Sexuality leaning towards the Line of Heart (see Figure 15A) indicates marital discord. The line rising towards the little finger (see Figure 15B) indicates good health for one's spouse. A broken line with islands or with two branches (see Figure 15C) shows obstacles in marital life or love relationships. More than one Line of Sexuality indicates a long period of fulfilment of sexual desires. Along with this, if the little finger is longer than normal and thick too, then excessive lines point to sexual relations with many.

The Line of Mars moving from within the Line of Life also indicates marital compatibility or discord (see Figure 15D). A clean Line of Mars points to good relations with one's life partner; a broken Line of Mars indicates marital discord.

***Lines of Children (see Figure 16)***

Vertical lines on the Mount of Venus (see Figure 16A) tell about the man's procreative powers. These are called the Lines of Children.

If there are islands in the line separating the thumb from the palm, then the person's fertility can be gauged (see Figure 16B).

If the lines on the wrist (Bracelet Lines) are raised upwards in a circle (see Figure 16C), then there is difficulty in bearing children.

To answer questions relating to the number of children a person will have, it is necessary to see the palms of both the husband and wife and in case of obstacles, both should be conveyed the remedies to overcome the obstacles.

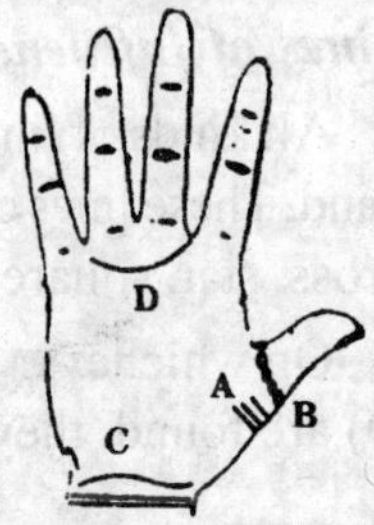

Fig. 16

***Girdle of Venus (Figure 16D)***

The circular line above the Line of Heart and below the mounts of Saturn and Sun is the Girdle of Venus. This line displays excessive emotionality. It also shows aggressiveness in sexuality if the palm is heavy and red. In a thin palm, this girdle indicates tension. If the Line of Heart is absent, then the Girdle of Venus should be considered as the inauspicious Line of Heart.

***Lines of Travel (Figure 17A)***

Answers to questions pertaining to travel are found in the lines on the Mount of Moon. Signs of travel for pleasure are not necessarily present on the palm, but if a branch of the Line of Life moves towards the Mount of Moon, then travels undertaken for the purpose of employment and business are likely.

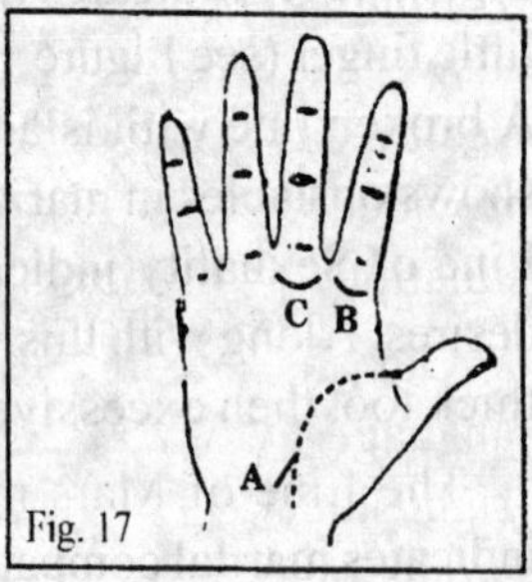

Fig. 17

To find out the time of travel, it is necessary to study the auspicious time at the Line of Saturn and its supporting lines. How to find out the auspicious or inauspicious time for travel will be explained later in this chapter.

***Ring of Solomon (Figure 17B)***

This line indicates one's inclination towards observing principles in life.

***Ring of Saturn (Figure 17C)***

This line is indicative of the characteristics of the Mount of Saturn, i.e. it conveys more of a tendency towards being a loner. A cross on the Mount of Saturn brings ill repute to a person.

***Lines of Influence (Figure 18)***

All kinds of lines—horizontal, diagonal, vertical are seen on the hand. These lines criss-cross to make symbols like an island, triangle, cross, star, square, trident, etc.

On whichever mounts the crosses, islands (18 A) and stars (18 D) are found, they convey the peculiar effects of the mounts. The square (18 E) reduces the adverse impact, while the triangle (18 B) and the trident (18 F) add to the advantages indicated by the mounts. A cross (18 C) or a star on the Mount of Jupiter proves auspicious.

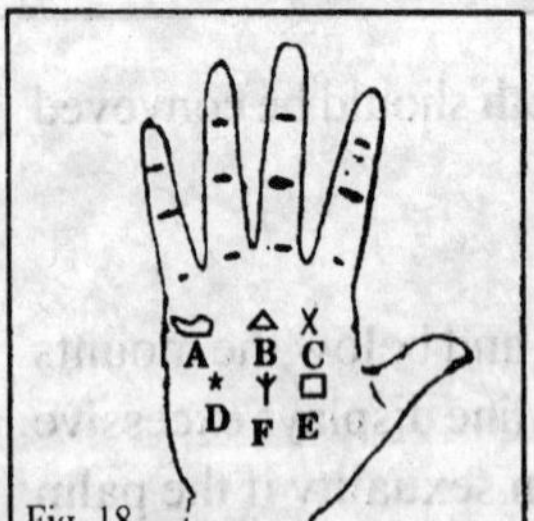

Fig. 18

***Axe Line/Parallel Line***

A line moving at some distance along the main line is called a Parallel Line. This line has the effect of accentuating the effect of the main lines. The Line of Sun and the Line of Mercury are lines parallel to the Line of Saturn. The Line of Mars runs parallel to the Line of Life. If the Line of Influence moves close to the main line, then it is called the Axe Line. The Axe Line reduces the effect of the main line.

## Removal of Certain Doubts

Many students at our Institute ask, "The Line of Saturn provides answers to queries pertaining to marriage, partnership, divorce, wealth, treasure, etc. Since answers to queries on these topics are provided by some other lines too, like the Line of Life, in such a situation, how are we to know what a particular line coveys?"

Our answer to such a question is that treat the lines like any language. Just as the meaning of the English word 'right' can be 'right side', i.e. opposite of left; or right or correct, i.e. opposite of wrong; or what is the person's authority; the choice of the word is decided by the reference to context. In palmistry, the answer to a question from the client is drawn according to the client's problem or question.

For instance, a person who is debt-ridden, for him auspiciousness of the triangle, square or good line conveys the freedom from debt; a person who wants love, marriage, divorce or employment, for him his auspicious sign conveys fulfilment of his desire while an adverse sign conveys obstacles as per his question.

In the second chapter of this book, predictions according to the handprints are made on the basis of the client's query or problem.

## Some Other Aspects to Remember

A person's basic nature can be judged from the length, width, thickness and the shape of the fingers along with the development or depression of the mounts on the hands. The effect of any person's basic nature is seen on his destiny too.

The lines of the palm predict the ups and downs in the person's life. Thick lines predict excessive struggle in life. Presence of too many lines on the palm indicates a state of mind that is faced with many options. Persons with few lines do not let their minds wander in different directions and they stay focused.

Persons with long fingers study deeply the issues that confront them. Their speed of doing work is slow. Persons with small fingers execute work at a faster speed.

People with long fingers are adept at planning while those with a broad palm believe more in taking action than in pondering over the actions taken.

A person with a thick hand has the ability to struggle and face problems. They can confront any problematic situation, while persons with thin hands tend to get tense in times of trouble.

Persons with hard hands are good in doing physical labour and firm in their views. Those who have supple skin on the hands, they mould themselves according to the demands of the situation.

The middle portion of the palm is normally depressed but if any part is excessively depressed, then the good effects of the lines running in that depressed portion are reduced.

To understand the reasons for the problems of the client, it is necessary to look at all these signs on the palm. It is easy to remove the obstacles if the reasons are understood initially itself.

**Should the Right Palm be Studied or the Left?**

Women who visit the Institute to get their future predicted, normally put forth their left hand. This is because since ancient times, it is believed that the left hand of the woman and the right of the man should be seen in palmistry, but according to research conducted by us, it is not desirable to make this differentiation between man and woman.

This is because, as per our belief, the lines on the hand are paths of electrical currents produced in the mind. According to medical science, the brain is divided into two hemispheres — the one on the left side of the brain affects the right hand and the one on the right side of the brain influences the left hand. The hand with which a person writes is more active and changes have been seen in the lines related to this hemisphere, i.e. if a person writes with the right hand, then changes are seen in the lines related to the left cerebral hemisphere.

After our long experience at studying palms, we have reached the conclusion that both the palms should be studied. If there are similar signs on both the palms, then the consequences of the lines should be taken with certainty but if there is a difference, then the signs on the hand used for writing should be given primacy.

## Rules to Predict the Good or Adverse Periods through Hand Lines

In our book, 'All the Secrets of Palmistry', I have written a full chapter on this subject. Instead of repeating the exposition over here, I want to convey that it is not possible to predict the exact dates of the events that occur in one's life. All that which can be predicted is during which period of life there is the possibility of an event occurring.

The Line of Life begins below the Mount of Jupiter and it ends near the wrist; hence the incidents of childhood should be checked where the Line of Life begins. The middle of the line reveals incidents that would have occurred during a person's youth. Incidents of old age are gauged from the state of the Line of Life at the wrist (see Figure 19). The rule related to age according to the Line of Life is relevant to the line running parallel to the Line of Life, i.e. Line of Mars.

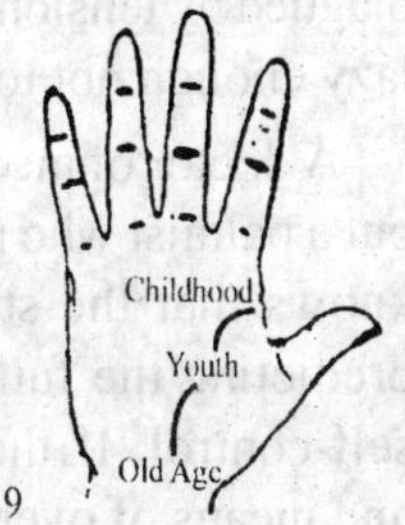

Fig. 19

The Line of Saturn begins near the wrist and ends on the Mount of Saturn (see Figure 20). Hence, the period of childhood can be gauged by observing the line near the wrist; the time of youth by the middle part and the period of old age according to the Mount of Saturn. The Line of Sun and the Line of Mercury are lines running parallel to the Line of Saturn. The rule for observing the Line of Saturn to find the age of a person is applicable to both these lines.

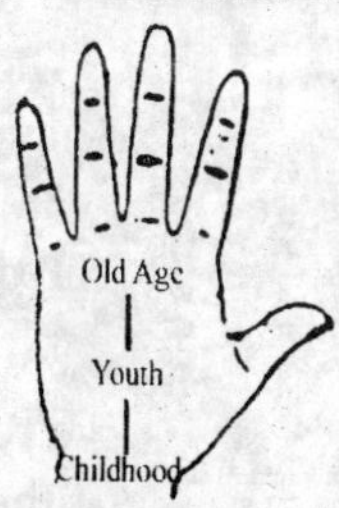

Fig. 20

## Queries Related to Death

Some people want to know the time of their death by showing their palms. The palm indicates if the person has some fatal disease or not and if the person on getting afflicted by a disease will have the vitality to overcome the disease or not. Telling more than this is against the ethics of the Institute. Life and death are in God's hands. To predict or to find out beforehand about death is to invite unnecessary worries upon yourself. It is better to do your work faithfully while accepting the presence of both God and death. When one's vigour decreases, one should make efforts to increase it by taking treatment and adopting measures so as to increase one's vitality and self-confidence.

**Future Outlook**

Prediction of one's future is a job of great responsibility. The palmist's predictions can add to the problems of a person already plagued by tension or it may increase his complacency, making him lazy enough not to take action and leave everything to Fate.

A doctor of medicine can provide the medicine to treat the body, but a palmist who predicts the future is a doctor of the mind, and he knows that the strength of the mind is limitless. Hence, when predicting the future, the palmist should exercise discretion and self-control. If there are obstacles, he/she should suggest ways and means of overcoming them.

# Predictions and Remedies

## *Chapter 2*

# Predictions and Remedies for 38 Handprints

### Introduction

In the book entitled **'Palmistry, How to Master It'** published by the Institute, we gave the handprints of 20 persons along with our predictions after making a general hand reading. In this current book, we make the predictions on the basis of each of our client's queries.

The predictions of only that hand are given which is in active use. By active hand we mean the hand with which the person writes. The reasons for the problems have been give of those persons whose handprints that have been included in the book. The words in which the reasons for a client's problems are conveyed depend upon the discretion of the person who is making the prediction.

The objective of the predictions made by the palmist is to increase the self-confidence of the already problem-ridden person. Keeping this aim in mind, apart from predicting, indications are given about the measures to adopt to counter the problems. Descriptions of the remedies to be followed are given in Chapter 4 of this book.

***Handprint No. 1***

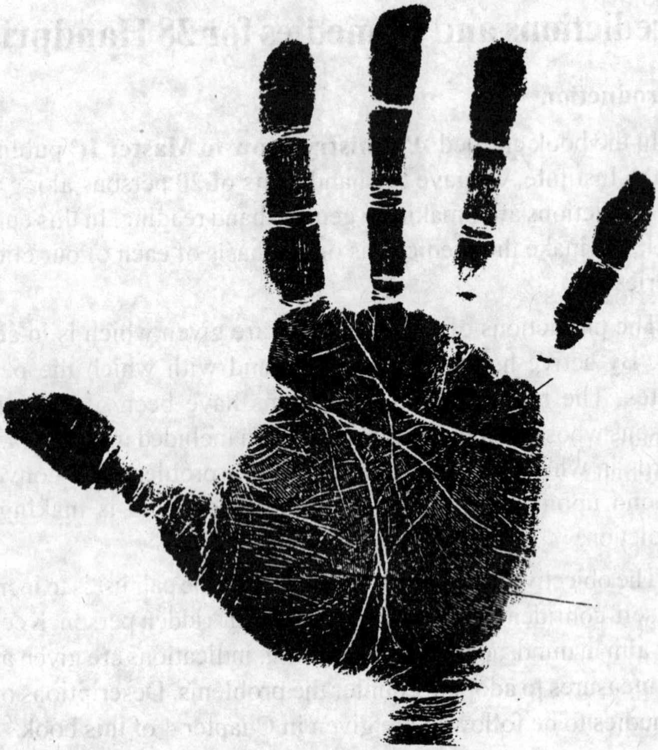

## Handprint 1: Prediction and Remedies

The handprint of this palm belongs to a 30-year old youth, who was working with his brothers in their family business. He wanted to know when he could branch out to start an enterprise of his own. On the basis of his question, we studied his palm.

His Line of Mercury emerges from an island at the age of 29. This island is at the confluence where the Life Line and the Line of Saturn merge. This conveys the presence of hurdles between the ages of 28 and 32 years.

Due to the emergence of the Line of Mercury, a new project can be undertaken at the age of 29 but till the age of 32, it would be a period of struggle. At the age of 35, a new Line of Saturn emerges from near the Line of Mercury and within that year itself, the Line of Desire emerges from the Line of Life to move towards the Mount of Mercury. Thus, after the age of 35, the person will witness expansion in his business. The trident on the Mount of Sun indicates that his old age will be passed in peace and happiness.

To locate the reasons for his problems, we looked at the little finger of our client. We find that this is at a considerable distance from the other fingers, indicating that the person has the tendency to impose his will upon others, as a result of which he is in constant conflict with his brothers, thus adding to his own tension. To get rid of his tension, we suggested the remedy that every morning he should concentrate on his little finger and pray to god or goddess by saying, "Give me the strength to tolerate the follies of others." A prayer offered from the heart will help reduce tension and provide comfort soon.

***Handprint No. 2***

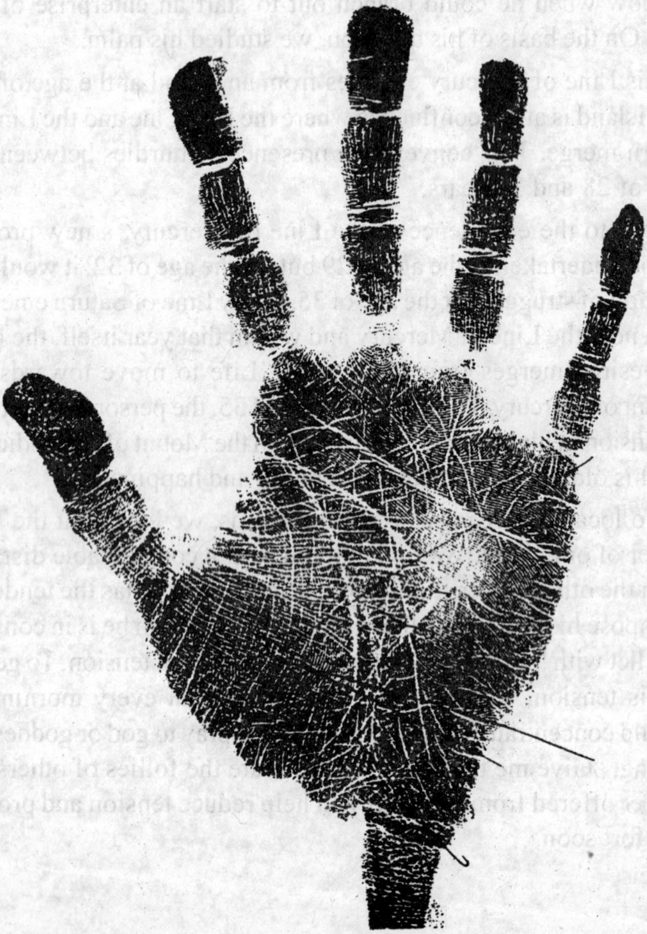

## Handprint 2: Prediction and Remedies

This handprint belongs to a 23-year old girl. She got married at the age of 22 and since then, she has been facing problems with her husband and tension with her family. The client's query is as to when she would find relief from her problems. According to her query, we decided to study her palm.

On first glance itself, we found the presence of too many lines on the hand. The main lines are thick and are criss-crossed by a series of lines of obstruction. The Line of Sexuality is inclined towards the Line of Heart.

To identify the cause for her tension, we find that the Line of Heart begins at the Mount of Jupiter and is twisted like a rope. Alongside is present a broken Girdle of Venus. The Mount of Jupiter is developed and a branch of the Line of Life goes towards the Mount of Jupiter and that there is a faint ring of Jupiter. It is obvious that the person is Jupiter-dominated. Despite this, she has worn a ring of pukhraj in her finger. This was equal to worsening her situation in life.

All the signs reveal that the person is excessively proud. A person with a long and thick Line of Heart is very sensitive and even a minor blow to her ego upsets her. Such persons are dissatisfied with whatever is available and feelings of love, friendship, enmity, etc. are present in a strong measure in them. All these signs point to the presence of conflicts and tension.

The client is asked to remove her pukhraj ring. To improve relationships, she is advised to wear an emerald ring on her little finger; to reduce tension, she is told to practice the simple yoga exercise of meditation (see the description of the mode of meditation in the fourth chapter of this book).

***Handprint No. 3***

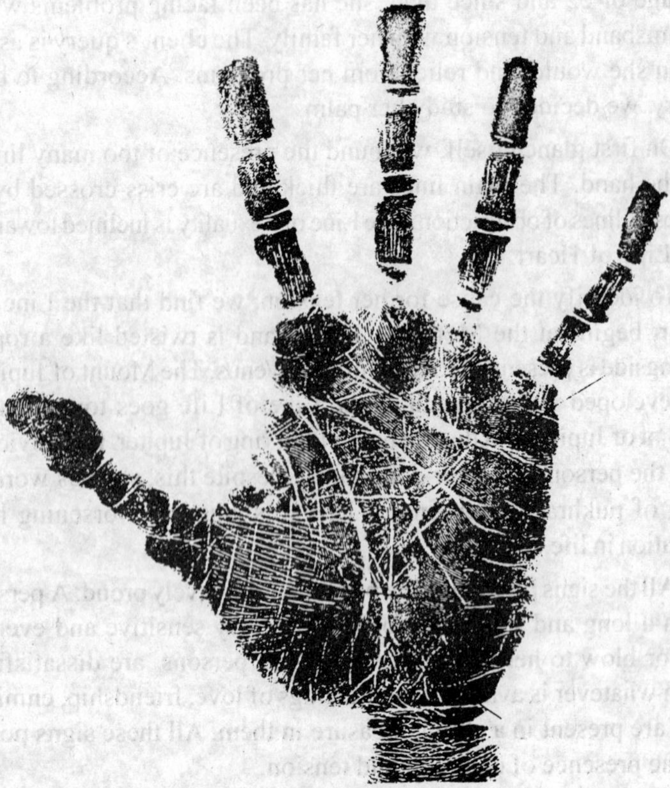

## Handprint 3: Prediction and Remedies

This palm belongs to a 37-year old youth, who was not satisfied with his job and wanted to start his own venture after leaving his service. His question was whether he should start on a business or look for a new job.

On studying his palm, we find that he has two Lines of Saturn on his palm: one emerges from the Mount of Moon or the Mount of Luna, while the other emanates from a branch of the Line of Life. Both arise at the age of 28. Both the Lines of Saturn end at the age of 37 years. One Line of Mercury emerges at the age of 31 years and along with it arises a thick Line of Mercury, which can be called the Axe Line. This Axe Line offsets the effects of the Line of Mercury and both these lines are stopped at the age of 40 years by the line of obstruction. After the age of 42 years, there is no auspicious sign on the palm. Hence, the youth is advised not to give up his regular job but try to concentrate his mind on his work.

On probing further, the person replies that he has already left his old job and the cause for his losing the job was the allegation of corruption levelled against him. To find out the reason for the allegation, we look at his little finger and find that it is longer than normal and crooked. To lessen the adverse impact of the little finger, we advise him to wear a pukhraj ring in his index finger, so that he may be discouraged from adopting the wrong path in his desire to become rich in a short time. He is also asked to start a small venture by investing some money and avoid taking undue risks.

***Handprint No. 4***

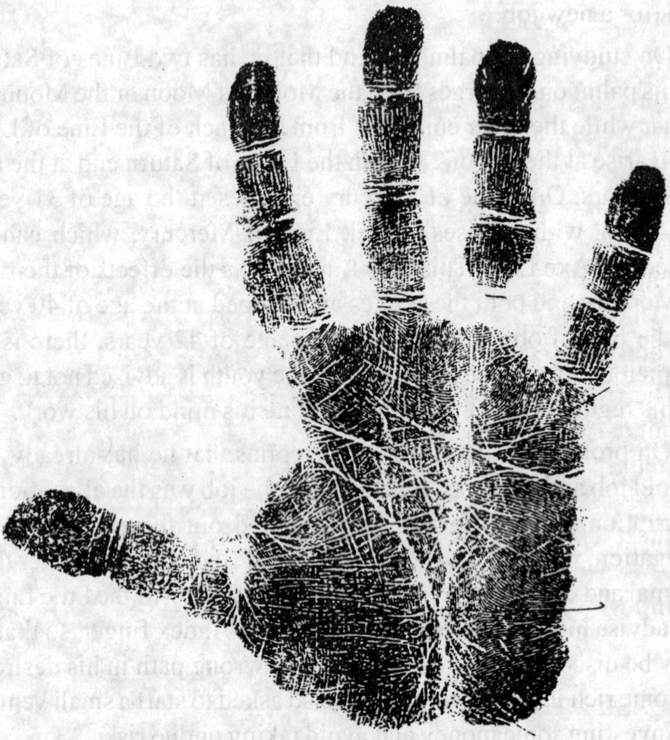

## Handprint 4: Prediction and Remedies

This palm belongs to a 47-year old middle-aged man who is debt-ridden. Apprehensive of losing his reputation, he remains tense and wanted to know if he would be able to keep his reputation intact or not.

The two rings of Jupiter on the Mount of Jupiter reveal that the person's first priority is his self-respect. There are many lines of obstruction that bisect the vertical lines of the Mount of Saturn and the Mount of Merçury. They signify loss of wealth. Now we try to identify the reasons for the hurdles in his path.

The space between the Line of Life and the Line of Head indicates that the client, in order to fulfill his desires, listens to no one. The longer-than-normal ring finger points to his nature of taking rash and risky decisions.

The auspicious sign is that among the three vertical lines on the Mount of Sun, two are without obstructions; hence, his reputation will remain intact. In order to curb his habit of taking rash decisions, he is advised to wear an iron ring in the middle finger and pray by reciting the sankat nivarak mantra (obstacle-removing mantra) daily. This way he would find rélief from problems (see the sankat nivarak mantra in the fourth chapter of this book).

***Handprint No. 5***

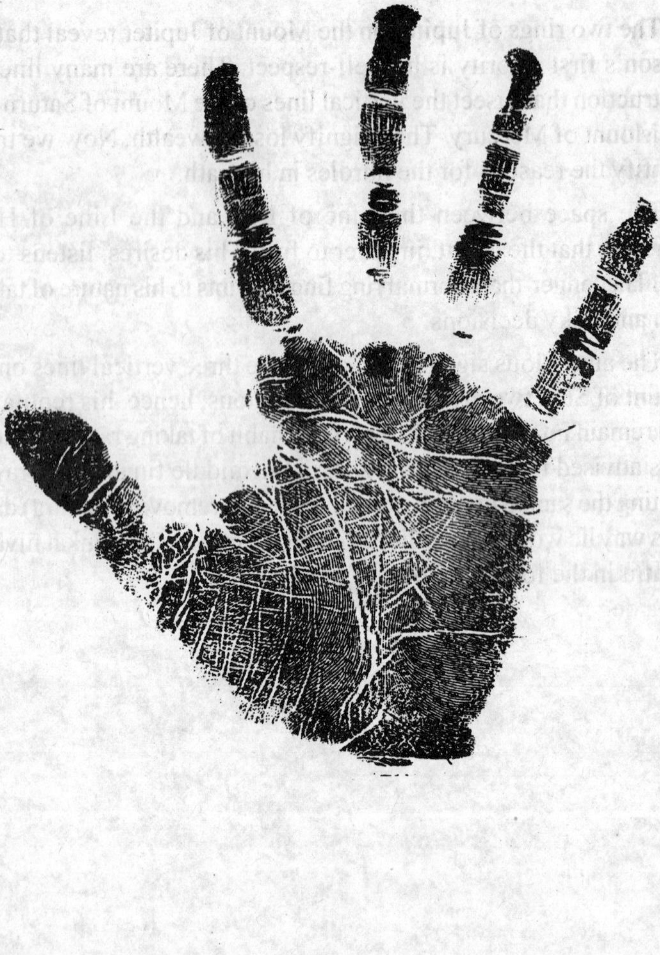

## Handprint 5: Prediction

This is the palm of a 29-year old youth, who was working in a transport business with his brothers. He had complaints against all his friends and relations. He wanted to know as to when he would succeed in life.

His Line of Heart is extra long and is broken into parts. He has a Girdle of Venus too. These signs indicate excessive sensitivity and emotionalism. His Line of Head is broken while his Line of Life is thick and straight. All the vertical lines are bisected by Lines of Obstruction. All the signs of being unlucky are present on this palm.

The ring finger, which is longer than the index finger, indicates impetuosity in taking decisions. To bring stability in him, he is advised to wear a ring of iron in his middle finger. He replies, "I don't want to wear any ring." As an alternative, he is told to wear clothes of blue colour, but he answers, "I do no like blue colour."

He is advised to practice digital exercises to remove negative traits in the Line of Head and the Line of Heart; but he fails to be convinced by these suggestions. He wants that some sort of *taveez* be given to him to wear — one that would make him rise high in life. It is expected of a person with such a Line of Head to make such a demand, but we were unable to fulfill his demand.

***Handprint No. 6***

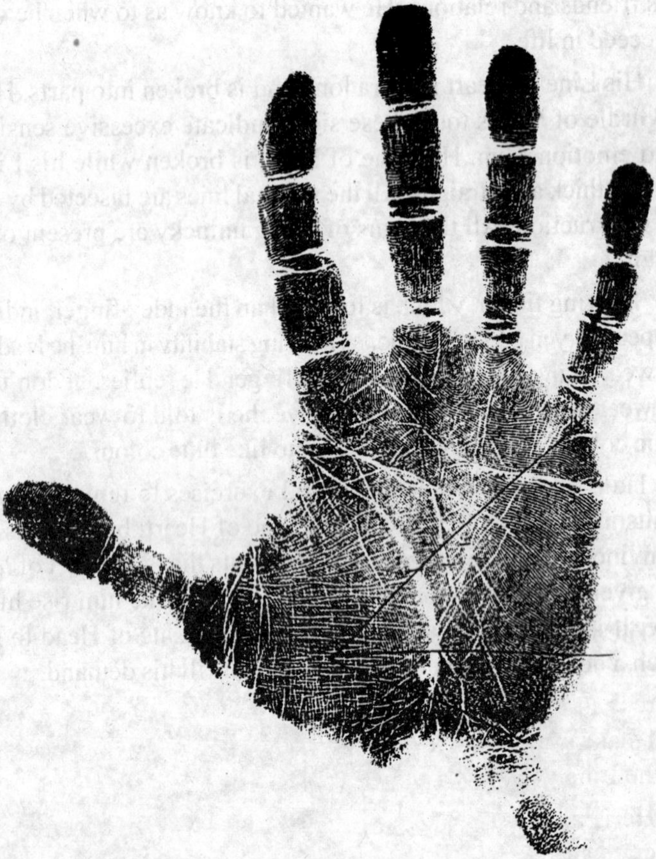

# Handprint 6: Prediction and Remedies

The palm belongs to a 34-year old youth who was married at the age of 26 years and divorced at the age of 32. The client's query was as to when he would remarry.

The Line of Sexuality is seen drooping down in the handprint, pointing to marital discord. The index finger is shorter than normal which keeps him free of criticism from others. There is space between the Line of Head and the Line of Life at the beginning, indicating the client's nature to do as he wishes.

From 29 to 40 years of age, the Axe Line is present with the Line of Mercury and the Line of Life grows thicker before reaching the wrist. All these signs point to family troubles continuing till the age of 60.

The client wants to know about his remarrying. To find the reply to his query, we observe a new Line of Saturn emerging from the Mount of Moon or the Luna Mount at the age of 31 before meeting the main Line of Saturn at the age of 40. It is learnt from the client that at the age of 31 years, he had fallen in love with a girl who his family members did not approve of but he wanted to marry her only.

The reply to the client's query is that he would get married at the age of 40 but he would not find happiness. The reason is that there is an island in the Line of Head that acts as a hurdle in helping him make the right decisions and also due to the gradual thickening of the Line of Life.

He is advised to wear a pukhraj ring in his index finger and practice anguli mudra (digital postures) to make his mind strong (description of the anguli mudra is given in the fourth chapter of this book).

***Handprint No. 7***

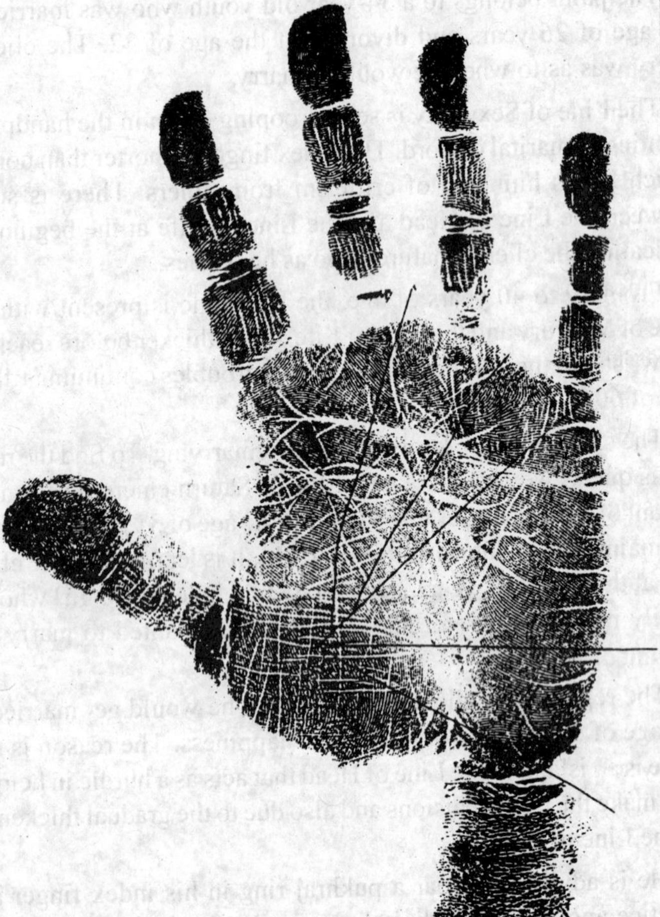

# Handprint 7: Prediction

This palm belongs to a 26-year old boy, who was dissatisfied with his marriage. He wanted to divorce his wife so as to marry again.

The Line of Sexuality droops down in the handprint, pointing to obstructions in married life. The Line of Heart is extra long, thick and broken. It appears from this that the client is extra-sensitive and holds great expectations from his wife and near and dear ones. His Line of Head is broken and short. This means that the person is incapable of making correct decisions. Even if such a person breaks the old bond to establish a new one, he cannot lead a happy married life.

The client had not come to find out about any remedies to adopt. He merely wanted to divorce and his desire for remarriage was very strong. On seeing his plans, effort was made to look for some auspicious signs.

The triangle close to the Line of Saturn between the age of 27 and 30 years and the emergence of the Line of Mercury from the Line of Saturn points that with the help of his wealth, he would immediately obtain divorce and at 30, he would be married again.

As he expressed no desire to find out the measures on how to lead a happy married life, hence no need was felt for suggesting any solutions to him.

*Handprint No. 8*

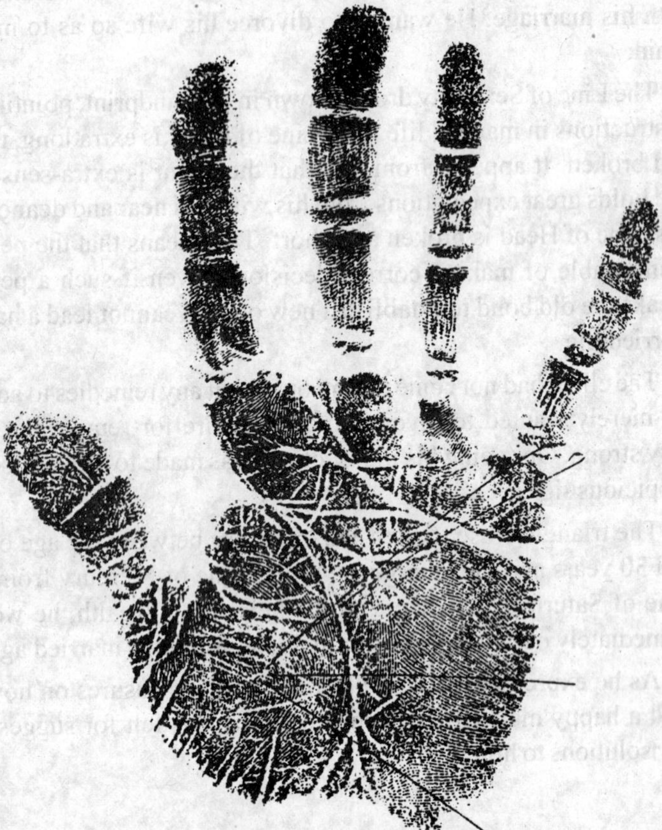

## Handprint 8: Prediction and Remedies

This palm belongs to a Class IV employee who was married in childhood. He had one a son and four daughters. To enhance his income, he used to do part-time service at different places in addition to attending his regular job. One daughter had been married off and his question was when his other daughters would be married.

The three major lines are thick which point to a troubled life. The Line of Head is short, indicating lack of wealth. The Line of Heart is long and its branch meets the Line of Head. With these lines intersecting each other, all kinds of squares and triangles are formed. This means that when problems would arise, doors to solving the problems would open simultaneously. Lines of obstruction are many but not even one of these lines obstructs the path of the main lines, thus after facing struggles, he would keep on succeeding.

A line of obstruction makes a triangle on top of the Line of Heart and along with it is present a square. After this, there is no line of obstruction.

The answer to the client's query is that he will face problems in getting his daughters married and his old age would be passed in comfort.

To ease the period of struggle, he is advised to daily recite the sankat nivarak mantra for removing obstacles (see the mantra in the fourth chapter of this book)

***Handprint No. 9***

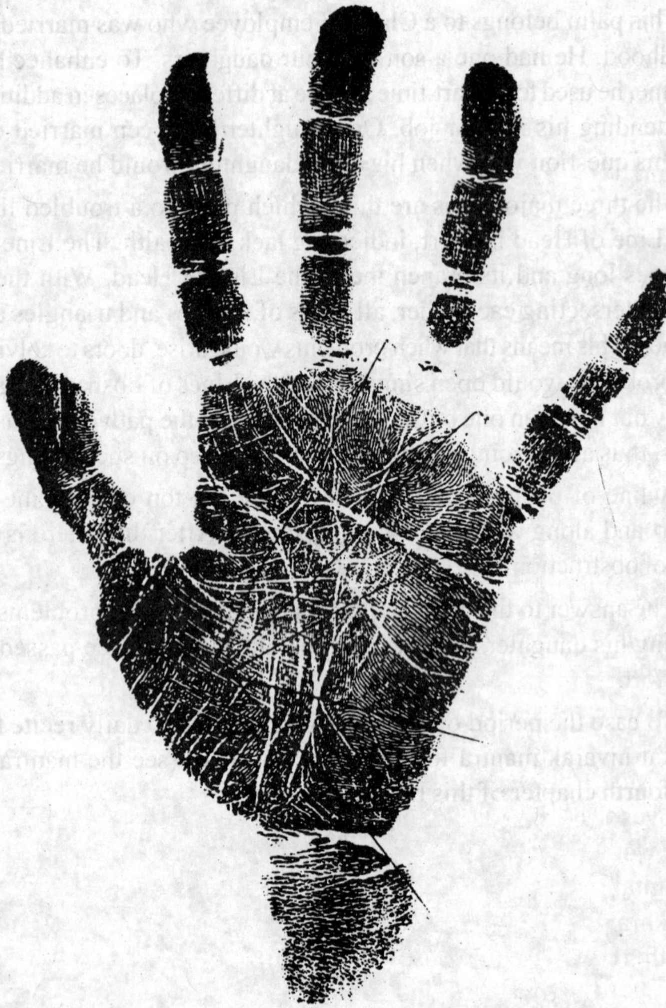

## Handprint 9: Prediction and Remedies

This is the palm of a 40-year old woman. Dissatisfied with her home and family, she wanted to take to a life of spiritualism. She wanted to know when her desire would be fulfilled.

At the age of 35 years, a line branches out from the Line of Saturn to move towards the Mount of Sun. This indicates the person's desire to earn fame. At the age of 42 years, this line is bisected at many points by lines of obstruction that create hurdles in the path of her desires. At 35 years, a new Line of Mercury arises to meet a branch of the Line of Head and makes a triangle. A beautiful trident is seen on the Mount of Mercury, on the Mount of Saturn and the Mount of Sun. According to these signs, at the age of 35 years, the seed of renunciation is sowed in the family. Till 42 years, there are lines of obstruction, but after 42 years, her desire to enter the life of spiritualism will be fulfilled.

Now let us try to find out the cause for the hurdles. A branch of the Line of Heart moves towards the Mount of Jupiter, indicating an overpowering desire to earn respect. The little finger is away from the other fingers, which creates hurdles in adjusting to the family. Both these signs show that the person does not get along with her family, making her turn to spiritualism. The effects of both these signs will remain even after adopting a life of spiritualism. On the Mount of Sun, at the age of 50 years, the line of obstruction proves the cause for her mentally disturbed state. To remove this, the woman is advised to practice heart-strengthening anguli mudra (digital postures) and meditate. She is also told not to wear any pukhraj (see the description of the remedies in the fourth chapter of this book).

***Handprint No. 10***

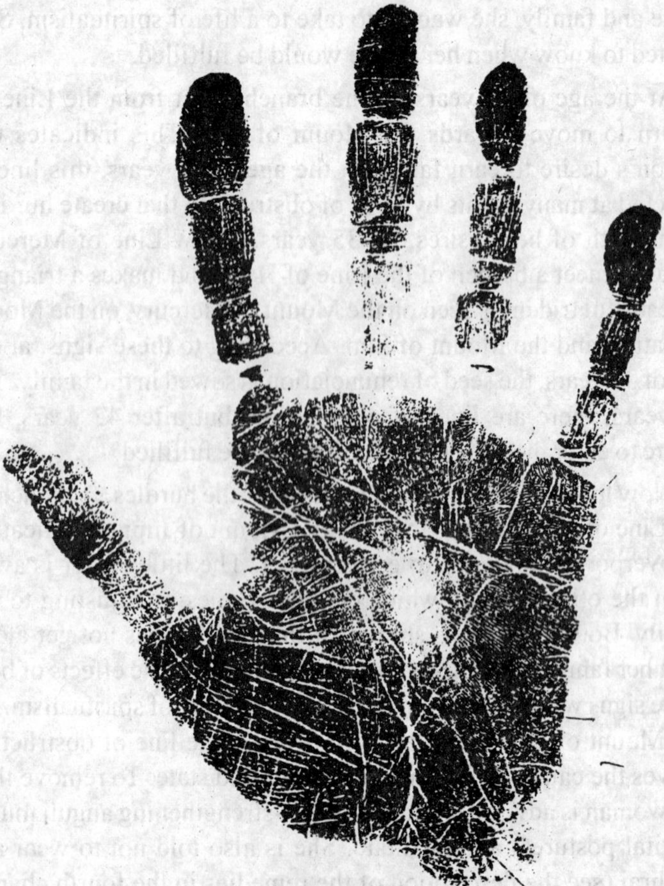

## Handprint 10: Prediction and Remedies

This palm belongs to a 27-year old boy who wanted to give up his job and start his own business.

In this palm, the Line of Head is short, indicating tension due to lack of wealth and restricted growth of the mind. The Line of Life is straight and has many islands. The portion on the Mount of Saturn that lies below the Line of Saturn is depressed till the age of 42. These signs point to gains after a life of great struggle.

The Line of Mercury is good. It stops at a particular spot at the age of 29 years. A new Line of Mercury emerges from a different spot to move clearly towards the Mount of Mercury. A small portion where the Line of Mercury intersects the Line of Heart is broken. Life after the age of 50 years passes smoothly and subsequently all the vertical lines are without obstruction on all the mounts. According to these signs, the answer to the client's query is that the ideal time for change of job is 29 years. Till 42 years of age, he will have to struggle hard to expand his business and subsequently there will be constant progress.

The Line of Head is short and the hand is wide. Because of this he will find more success in work involving physical labour. Work calling for use of the mind is not suitable for him. To alleviate his struggles, he is advised to practice strength-imparting anguli mudra (digital postures) and also brain-stimulating mudra or postures (see the description of both the mudras in the fourth chapter of this book).

*Handprint No. 11*

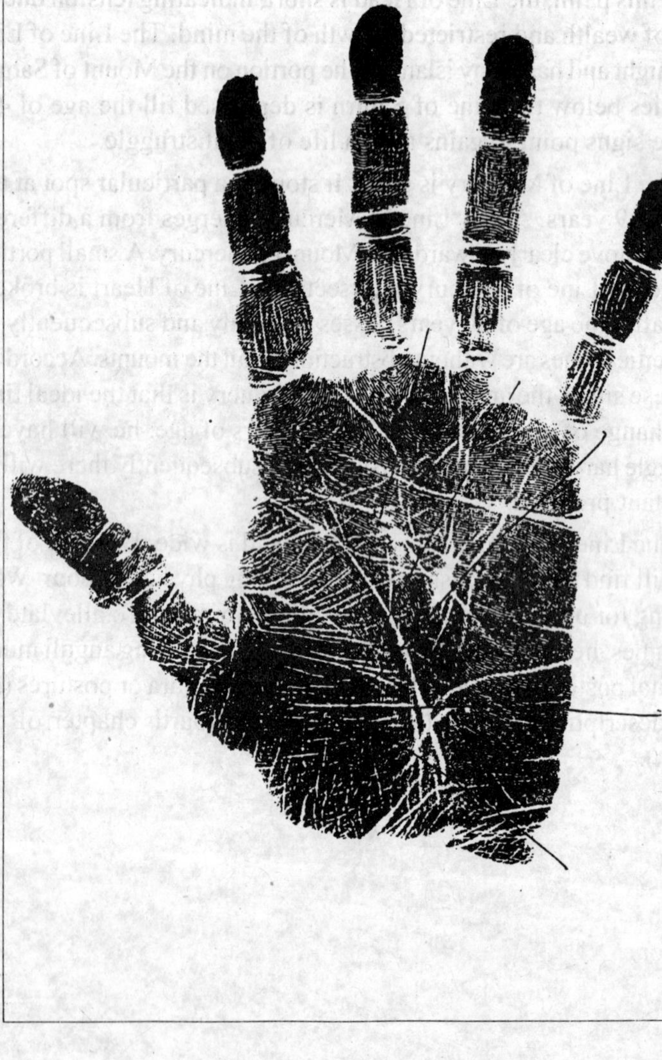

## Handprint 11: Prediction and Remedies

This is the handprint of a 28-year old youth working in the family's building construction business. He wanted to separate and branch out into his own export business.

The Line of Head of the client emerges away from the Line of Life. A second Line of Head arises in the form of a branch of the Line of Life. Both the Lines of Head are defective, indicating a mind in a perpetual state of dilemma and unable to reach any decision.

The ring finger is longer than normal, showing a tendency to be rash and take hasty decisions.

At the age of 29 years, the Line of Saturn halts within the Line of Life. A Line of Influence emerges from here to move towards the Mount of Sun and two lines of obstruction arise above this Line of Influence at the age of 30, while the Line of Saturn turns towards the Mount of Sun.

All these signs indicate that the person will leave his family business at 28 years of age and benefit from conducting business abroad, though defects in the Line of Head will not let him succeed fully. At 35 years of age, the Line of Sun emerges from a depression. At the same time, the Line of Desire emanates from the Line of Life and after the age of 42, all the three lines — Mercury, Sun and Saturn — become free of defects.

The client is advised to start a new export-import business with a small capital. The period between 35 to 42 years will be full of struggle and to escape from this, he is advised to practice anguli mudra (digital postures) for strengthening his brain.

To exercise control over his rash behaviour, he is advised to wear an iron ring in his middle finger. After the age of 42, he could go in for expanding his business enterprise.

***Handprint No. 12***

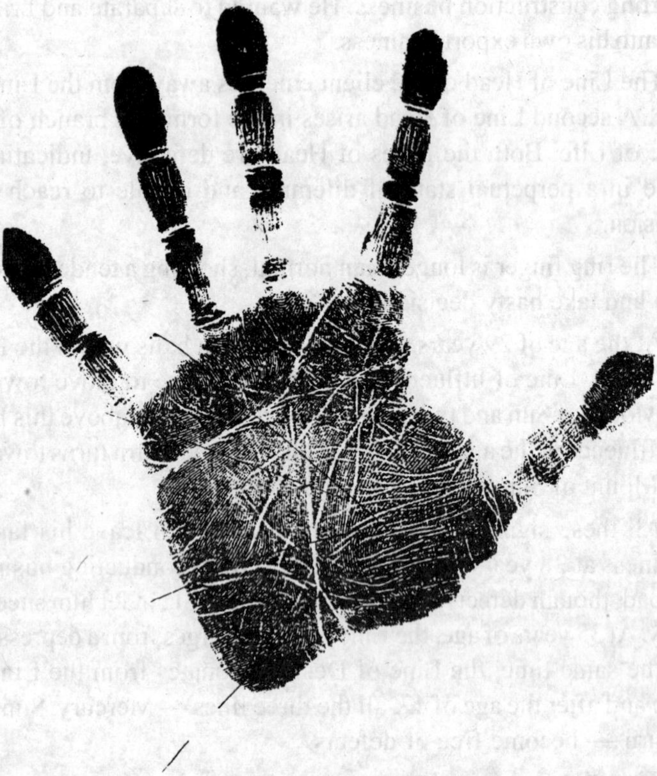

## Handprint 12: Prediction and Remedies

This hand belongs to a 37-year old youth who was fighting for divorce from his wife. On acquiring freedom from this marriage, he wanted to marry some other woman. His query was as to when he would get married again.

The Line of Sexuality is branched, indicating hurdles in marital relations. A branch of the Line of Heart moves towards an island in the Line of Head and after this island, the Line of Head tilts towards the Mount of Luna, leaving space between the points where the Line of Life and Line of Head emerge. These signs indicate that the client is self-willed and keeps spinning webs of impossible dreams. In all probability because of this nature of his, he is unable to get along with his first wife.

The client had not come to listen about his shortcomings and therefore, his faults were not pointed out. His question was when he would remarry and the answer to this was available in two signs — one, at the age of 42, his Line of Saturn halts at the Line of Head and from another spot on the Line of Head, a second Line of Saturn emerges. From the age of 42 onwards, a branch from the Line of Life running parallel to the Line of Saturn emanates to move towards the Mount of Jupiter and after crossing an island on the Line of Head, it reaches the Mount of Jupiter.

These signs signify that the right age for remarriage is 42 years. This apart, all the signs indicate that the second marriage will continue for 50 years, after which the client will renounce the world on losing interest in life. This is because the second Line of Saturn ends on the island on the Line of Heart at the age of 50, and the line emerging from the Line of Life on turning after the island on the Line of Head moves towards the Mount of Jupiter.

***Handprint No. 13***

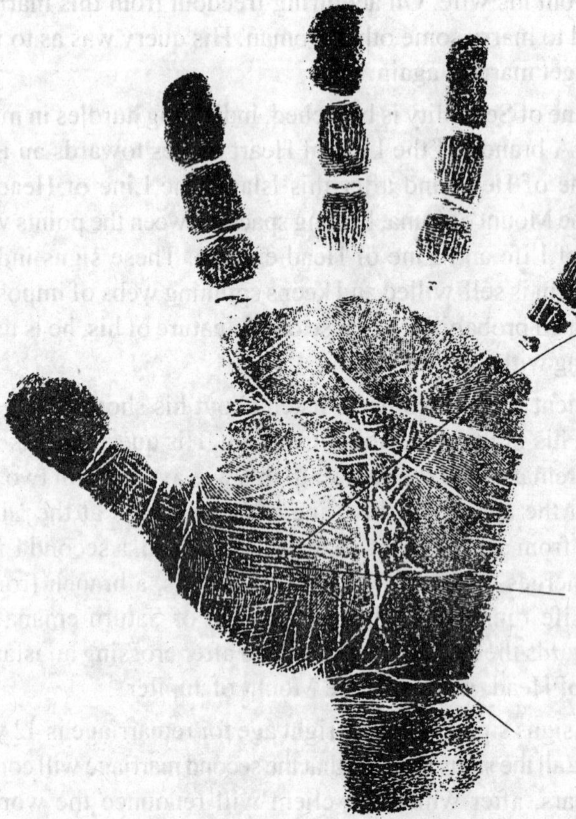

## Handprint 13: Prediction and Remedies

This hand belongs to a client desirous of becoming the head of a muth (religious establishment). At the time of showing his palm, his age was 22 years. His query was that after the death of the current head of the muth, would he possibly be appointed the next head to the post.

His palm is broad which reveals his nature of being extra active. The fingers are short and the ring finger is longer than normal, indicating the tendency to know the results immediately after every assignment is completed by him.

Between the ages of 23 and 30 years, an island touching the Line of Saturn is an obstruction in fulfilment of his desires. After the age of 30, the Line of Saturn on becoming free, moves towards its destination and the Line of Mercury emerges in this period. Hence, the age for becoming the religious head is 30 years. At the age of 32 years, a Line of Influence emanates from the Defensive Mars to meet the Line of Saturn at the age of 40 years. This announces the establishment of some external sextual contact. After this Line of Influence meets the Line of Saturn, the Line of Mercury emerges at another spot and halts at the age of 38 years when lines of obstruction bisect the Line of Saturn.

Where the Line of Mercury stops, a new Line of Sun emerges from another spot. This is a sign indicating destruction of the effects of the lines of obstruction. The answer to the client's query is that the age for becoming the head of the muth is 30 years and the time for finding relief from hurdles is 38 years.

To exercise control over his rash decisions and take action with a cool mind, the client is advised to wear an iron ring in his middle finger and refrain from wearing a coral or any red stone.

***Handprint No. 14***

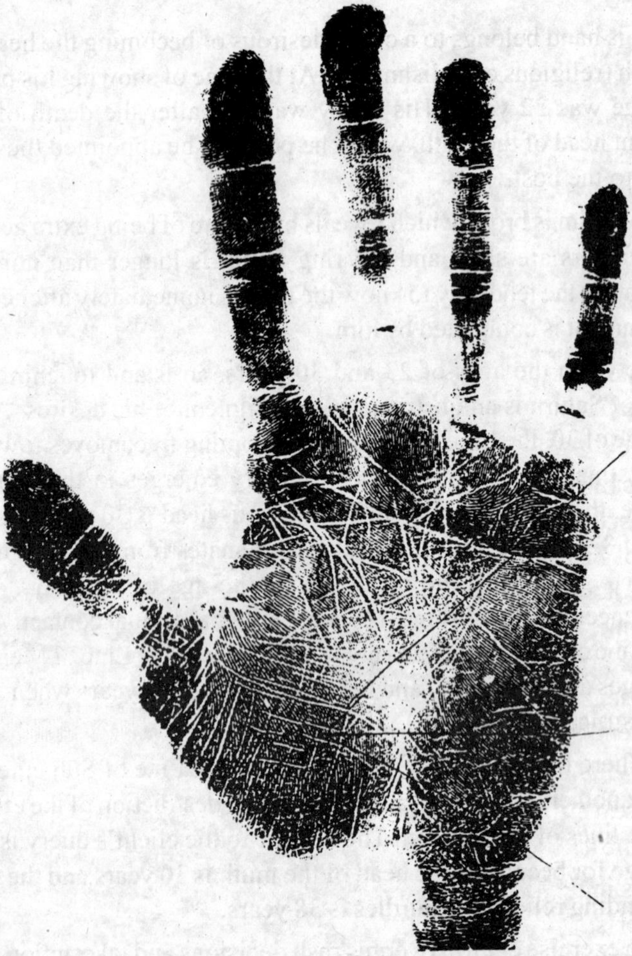

## Handprint 14: Prediction

The mother of a 28-year old boy came to our Institute with her son. The son sat quietly, while the mother complained about her son that he constantly kept on changing his jobs and thus was not successful in life. He even refused to get married, as he wanted to renounce the world and become a sadhu (an ascetic). She was curious to know as to when he would get married.

The hand is heavy. The Mount of Venus is pronounced and the Line of Sexuality is extremely long and branched. The Line of Heart is extremely long and the Girdle of Venus is present. These signs indicate presence of strong sexual desires. Despite this, the son was refusing to marry and wanted to become a sadhu. Efforts to find out the cause for this attitude had to be made now.

His Line of Head is short and is bisected by a line of obstruction. Islands are present on the Line of Life till the age of 30 years. The Line of Saturn joins the Line of Life till the age of 30 years, after which it emanates as the Line of Desire. A new Line of Saturn is seen emerging as its parallel from the Mount of Moon. Prior to that, since 28 years of age, a Line of Mercury emerges from the Line of Life. Hence, from a normal point of view, the time for his marriage is between 28 and 30 years but the son was refusing to get married.

The mother is advised separately that the son is going to enter into a free sexual relationship as he does not wish to take on the responsibility of a wife and children. Obviously he is a spoilt son of a rich mother.

His interest lies neither in employment nor in business. On his mother's insistence he has joined the business, but due to lack of interest, the business incurred losses. He has no intention of becoming a sadhu.

The mother is advised not to marry off the son against his wishes, as his wife would not remain happy. The inability to see her daughter-in-law and grandson made the mother unhappy. Hence, to provide comfort to her heart, the mother is advised to pray to her family god or goddess that her son may soon acquire some good sense.

***Handprint No. 15***

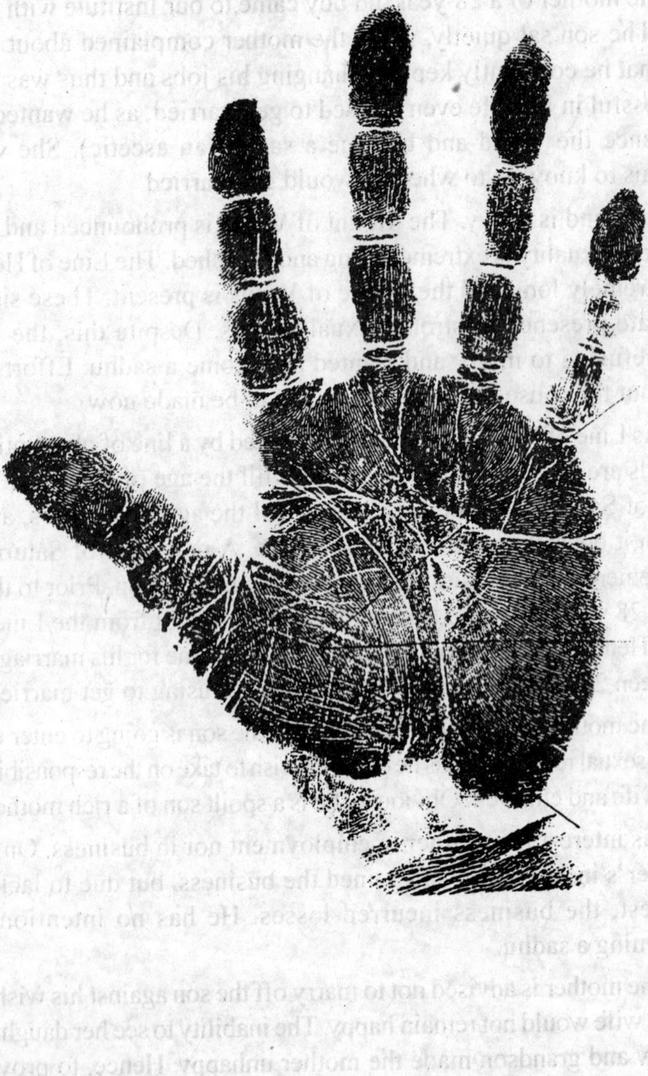

## Handprint 15: Prediction

This hand is of a 67-year old middle-aged man. On seeing his short Line of Life, some palmists had predicted that he would die soon. To remove his fears, he had visited our Institute to show his palm to us. The client was a translator in the Lok Sabha. After retirement he had become a free-lance translator.

According to the length of his Line of Life, he should have died at the age of 52 years. He is then told that the short Line of Life signifies family discord after the age of 52 years and this he readily accepted. Two long Lines of Mars substitute for the short Line of Life. The Line of Head is abnormal. Moving till the centre on its path, it gets lost on the Line of Saturn. The remaining portion of this line reappears from the Line of Saturn.

The Line of Heart tilts down to occupy the place of the Line of Head, thereby offsetting the effects of the short Line of Head.

The vertical lines standing in the form of a trident on the three fingers point to a peaceful old age. The man needed no advice. It was enough to rid his mind of his apprehension about a short Line of Life.

***Handprint No. 16***

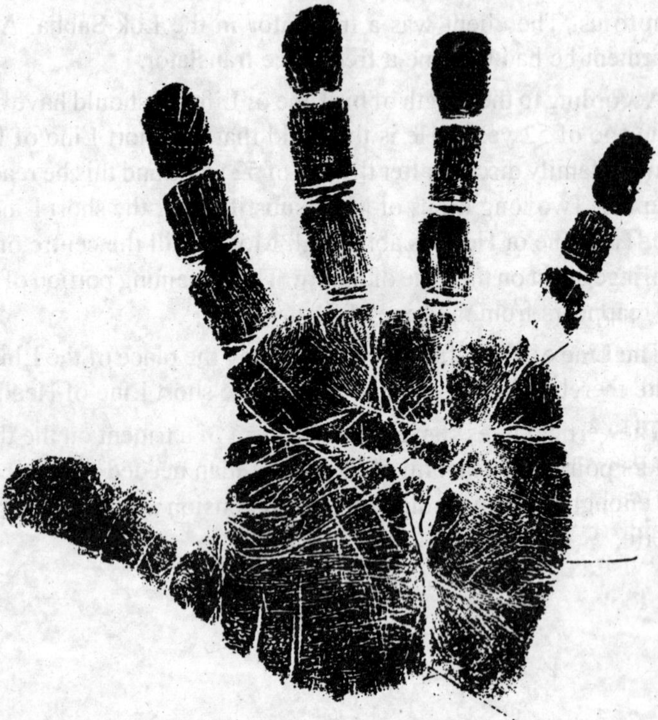

## Handprint 16: Prediction and Remedies

This is the hand of a 74-year old man. His Life Line too is short but the Line of Mars makes up for this shortcoming. He is unhappy with his sons and daughters-in-law and this fact is revealed by a short Line of Life. The problem of the client is that with great hardships he had brought up his children but now no one was bothered about him. His question was if he would ever find happiness and peace.

His Line of Head is thick, the Line of Heart is thick and between the two lines lie depressions in palm which indicate a life of struggle and blows to the heart. The hand is heavy and broad, revealing his ability to work hard and be resistant.

The vertical lines standing above the Line of Heart till the base of the fingers indicate that his old age would be without problems. The client is a believer of Sikh religion. Effort is made to convince him that no matter how tough his youth had been, his old age would be peaceful and happy. To decrease his mental tension, he is advised to read daily the guruvani called 'Sukhmani' from the Guru Granth Sahib (the religious scripture of the Sikh community) and keep busy by visiting the gurudwara regularly and taking up the responsibility of looking after the shoes of the devotees visiting the gurudwara.

***Handprint No. 17***

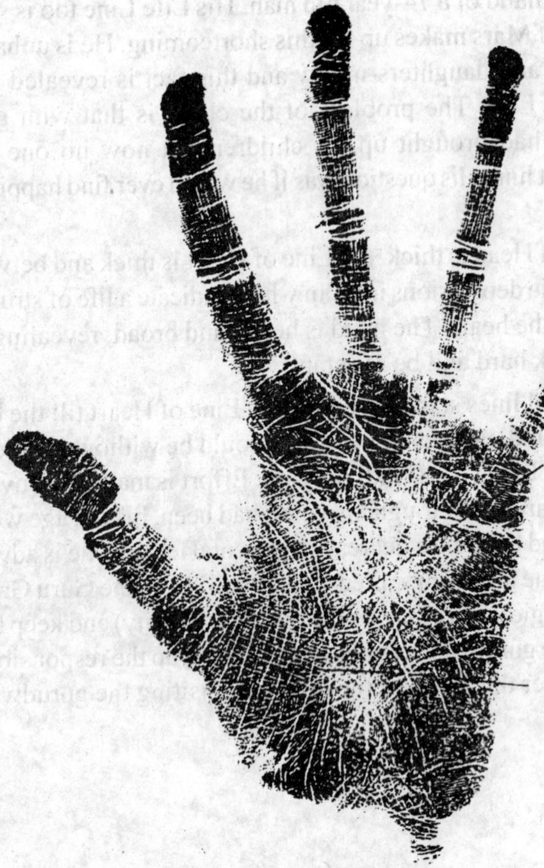

## Handprint 17: Prediction and Remedies

This hand belongs to a 16-year old girl, whose mother was worried about her health. To find the answer on how and when her health would improve, the mother and daughter had come to us.

A long and thin hand with long and knotted fingers and a long second phalange are seen on the thumb. All these signs indicate the client's limited physical strength but reveal a strong mental ability.

On studying her hand lines, the Line of Heart emanates like a chain with a tassel. On top of this is the Girdle of Venus. Her Line of Life and Line of Head are defective and full of islands till the age of 21. All the mounts are underdeveloped. These signs indicate that the girl keeps her thoughts to herself and thus remains tension-ridden.

The faults of the Line of Life and Line of Heart would disappear at the age of 21 years, proving feasible to her health. But, to improve the period prior to this, she is advised to adopt the following measures:

- She is strictly advised not to wear a neelam (blue sapphire ring) or an iron ring.
- She is told to wear a coral ring in her ring finger and a pearl ring in her little finger.
- She is told to acquire training in fine arts like music, literature, painting, etc.
- She must practice meditation daily (the method for meditation is given in the fourth chapter).

The girl is advised that by following the suggestions given above her health would definitely improve before the age of 21 years.

***Handprint No. 18***

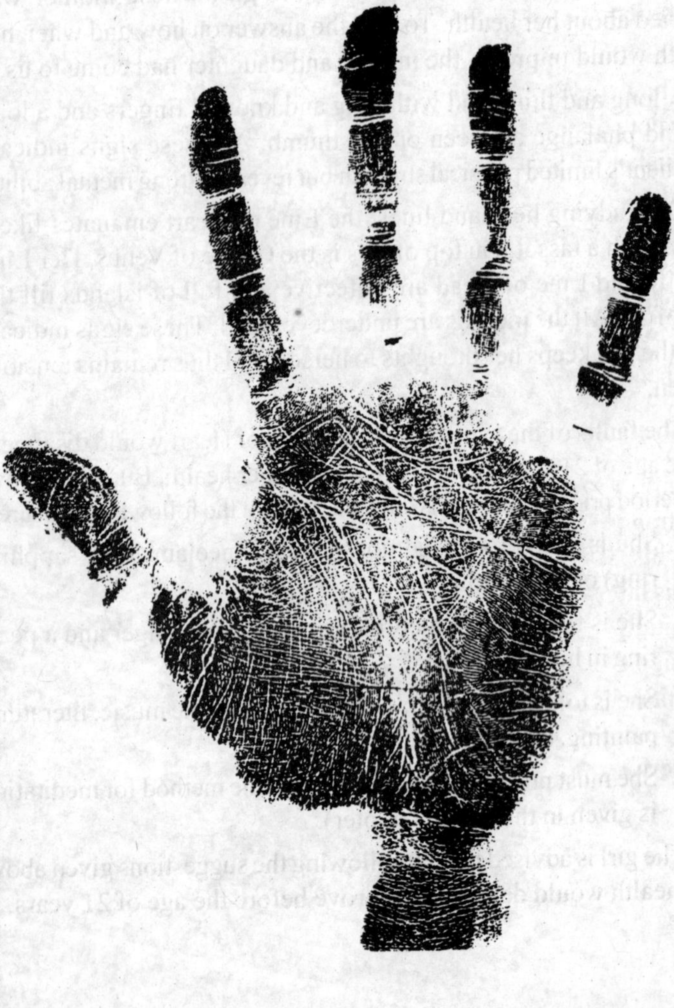

## Handprint 18: Prediction and Remedies

This hand is of a 22-year old boy who studied in a college. He had fallen in love with a girl in his class. Later, the girl left the city and his question was if he would ever meet the girl again.

The little finger is shorter than normal which indicates that he does not possess a practical nature. The entire Line of Life is dotted with islands. Branches of the Line of Heart tilt towards the Line of Head and the Girdle of Venus is made up of pieces. The Line of Head is short and its source is riddled with islands. Innumerable Lines of Sexuality are present. The Line of Saturn emerges from the Mount of Moon for 22 years and is broken into pieces after that. All these signs convey that the client's heart rules over the head and he is a person who carries his heart on his sleeves. There is no stability in his love.

At 27 years of age, the Line of Desire emerges from the Line of Life. At 30 years of age, its branches are seen trying to repair the fragmented or broken Line of Mercury. The boy is advised to turn his attention away from his girl friend; wear an emerald ring on his little finger; practice for five minutes daily all the anguli mudra (digital postures) to strengthen his heart, mind and make his life tension-free. The suitable age for his marriage is 27 years. To maintain marital harmony, the above-mentioned solutions would prove beneficial and he would find release from tension. Descriptions of all these suggestions are given in Chapter 4.

*Handprint No. 19*

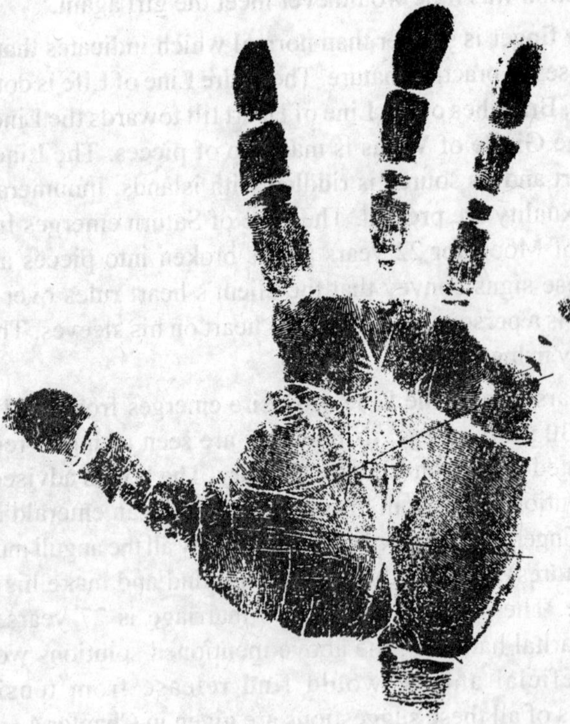

## Handprint 19: Prediction and Remedies

This hand belongs to a 30-year old youth who lived with his siblings in a joint family. To get away from family troubles, he wanted to establish a separate household. His question was as to when he would find such an opportunity.

A considerable portion of the Line of Heart, the Line of Head and the Line of Life is thick, indicating a life of struggle. A thick Line of Saturn emerging from within the Line of Life becomes free at the age of 30 years. But his parallel Line of Mercury is very thick, which is decreasing its impact.

At the age of 34 years, a pretty Line of Desire emanates from the Line of Life and after 41 years, the Line of Saturn, that had been emerging from before, crosses the Line of Head to move towards the centre of the Mounts of Saturn and Sun. The Line of Saturn above the Line of Heart and the Line of Sun are devoid of hurdles.

The answer to the query is that he would establish his own home at 34 years and subsequently he would consistently rise high. To improve the period till then, he is advised to wear a ring of iron in his middle finger. This is because the Ring finger and the little finger are longer than normal, indicating a over cleverness and hasty nature. The iron ring will put a brake on these tendencies and his struggles would lessen.

***Handprint No. 20***

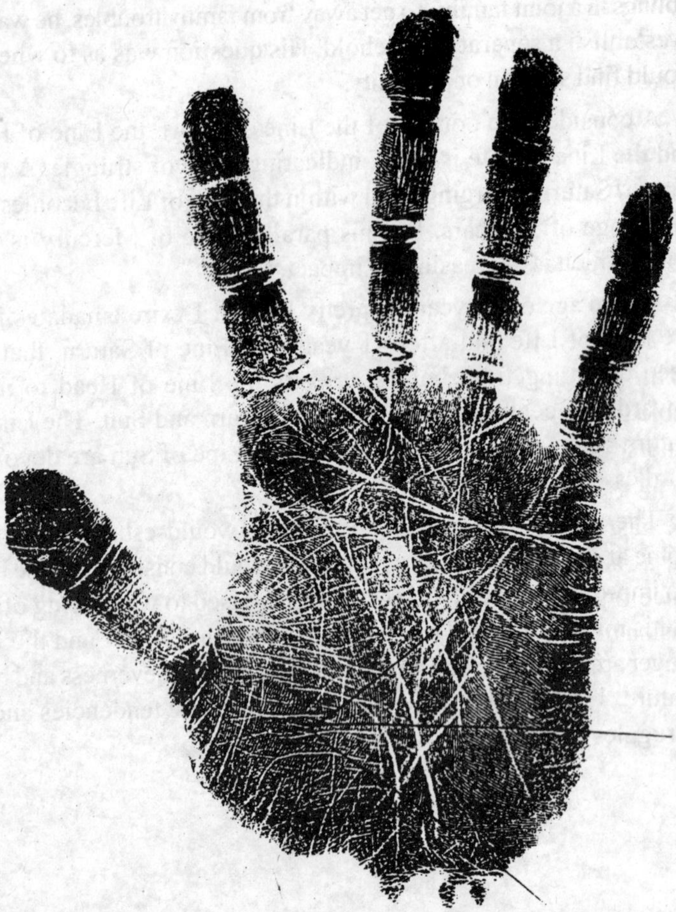

## Handprint 20: Prediction and Remedies

This hand belongs to a 36-year old youth, who was engaged in his own business since long. He wanted to start an export business in partnership with somebody.

The broad hand points to his being very active. The Line of Life moves towards the Mount of Moon or the Luna Mount. Innumerable lines emerging from within and outside the Line of Life carve out many fish lines that are in favour of foreign trade.

All the lines, like the Line of Saturn, Line of Mercury and the Line of Sun, are present. At places, these are crossed by lines of obstruction but none of them are able to stop the main lines. These are signs of success after a period of struggle.

The little finger is longer than normal, hence the partner will not be able to deceive him. Thus it is advisable for him to enter into a partnership to start foreign trade.

The longer-than-normal ring finger points towards a tendency to be hasty and rash. To overcome this tendency, he is advised to wear a ring of iron in his middle finger. With this, there is every chance of his exercising control over his nature of taking rash decisions, thus countering all the obstructions.

***Handprint No. 21***

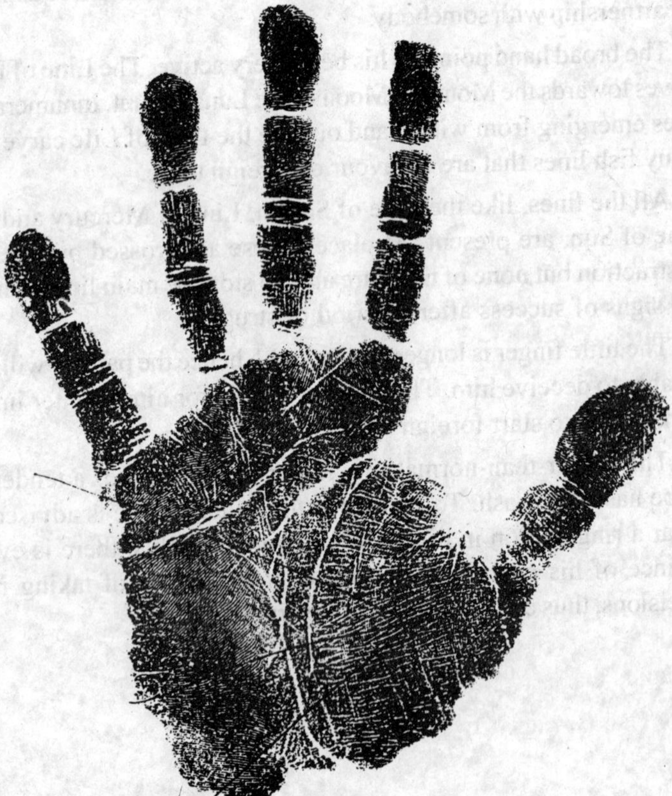

## Handprint 21: Prediction and Remedies

This hand is of a 32-year old youth who wanted to separate out from his family business and start his own venture. To emerge from this state of uncertainty, he visited the institute to show his palm.

The Line of Saturn on this palm has islands between the age of 31 and 36 years. His Line of Head is short. Hence, leaving his joint family business to start a new enterprise is not feasible.

He is advised to begin planning his own business by the age of 36 years. To find out his future, many vertical lines are seen by us over the Line of Head and the Line of Heart. These lines point to his inability to make up his mind on anything. He may not succeed despite the efforts that he puts in. To overcome his shortcomings, the client is advised to adopt the suggestion given below:

- Practice anguli mudra (digital postures) every morning to strengthen his brain.
- Every morning, practice tratak (stare unblinkingly at any object/subject) at base of finger and pray to God, requesting, "Give me the strength to be stable in my aim."

On adopting these measures at the earliest possible, the defects shall be removed and fortune may smile upon him (the method of tratak is given in the fourth chapter).

***Handprint No. 22***

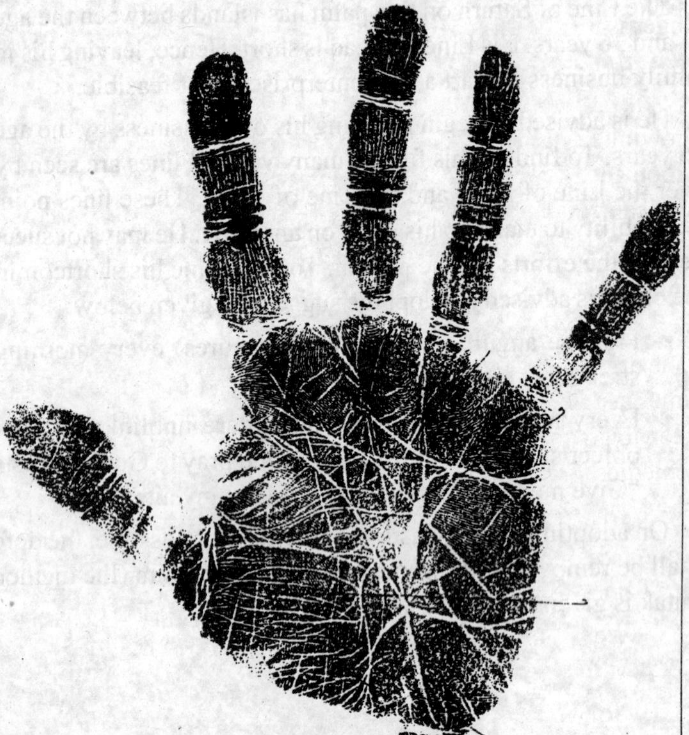

## Handprint 22: Prediction and Remedies

This hand belongs to an executive who heads a large company. His age was 42 years and he was unmarried, though he seemed keen to get married.

The hand is heavy and broad. The fingers are thick and the little finger is too far away from the other fingers. Too much distance is seen from where the Line of Life and the Line of Head arise.

All these signs draw a picture of a dictator. A horizontal line showing lack of control over one's feelings is seen on the Mount of Moon and this line with the Line of Sexuality tilt towards the Line of Heart that is broken.

A line acting as the bridge between the Line of Heart and the Line of Head is an obstruction to a happy marital life.

At the age of 42 years, the Line of Desire emanates from the Line of Life. It halts at age of 55 years. It is obvious that the marriage time has come but bond will not last long. But the client seems keen to get married. To make his marriage a success, the following remedies are suggested for implementation:

- To keep the mind cool, wear a ring of iron in the middle finger.
- Desist from wearing a coral so that the effect of dictatorship does not increase.
- Wear a pearl ring on his ring finger to counter the ill effects of the Mount of Moon.

By following these remedies, there is a likelihood of stabilising his married life.

***Handprint No. 23***

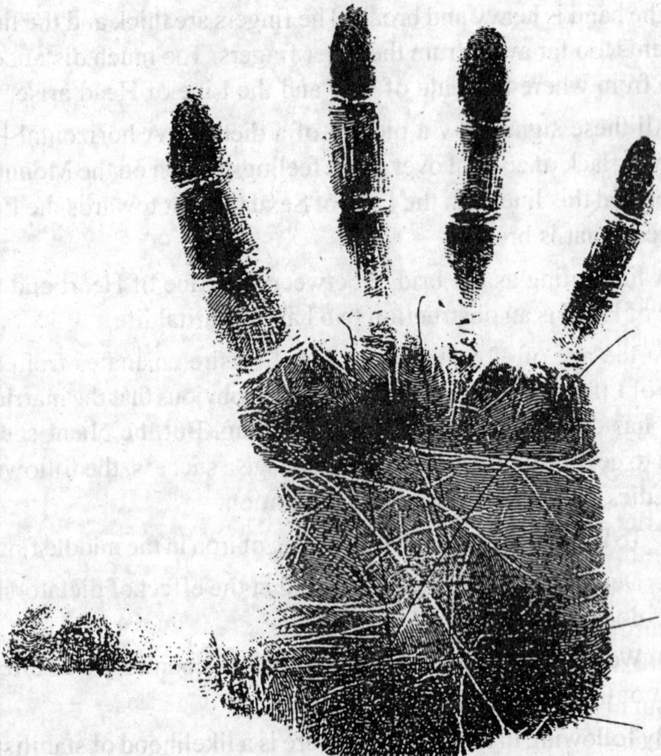

## Handprint 23: Prediction and Remedies

This hand belongs to a 38-year old woman who holds a high repute in the field of fine art. She had separated from her husband. Her question was whether she would reconcile with her husband or if she would meet some other man.

The Mount of Jupiter is strong and the Line of Life emerges from close to the Mount of Jupiter. This is a sign of the woman being very proud. The Line of Heart is defective, conveying excessive sensitivity. The ring finger is longer than normal, pointing to rashness and risk-taking tendencies. With these signs there is a possibility of the client having grievances against her spouse.

The Line of Saturn stops at the age of 38 years and at a small distance away, a new Line of Saturn emanates. At this very time, a branch (Line of Desire) of the Line of Life emerges. This period indicates a love affair or marriage to a new person, but both these stop on bisecting the line of obstruction and before reaching the Line of Head (at 46 years). This means that the marriage or the love affair will not last long.

After a short distance, a new Line of Saturn emerges from the Line of Head. This line goes to the Mount of Saturn and a trident is formed with many lines seen on the Mount of Sun. This means that the third relationship will continue for long, bringing in its wake both wealth and fame.

But all this is conveyed to the client in a roundabout a manner so that instead of solemnising the second relationship into a marriage, it would be advisable for her to keep it confined to a love affair.

To remain tension-free, the client is advised to follow the following remedies:

- Practice anguli mudra(digital postures) for strengthening the heart.
- Never wear a pukhraj ring.
- To become free from the effects of an extra long ring finger, wear a ring of iron in the middle finger.

***Handprint No. 24***

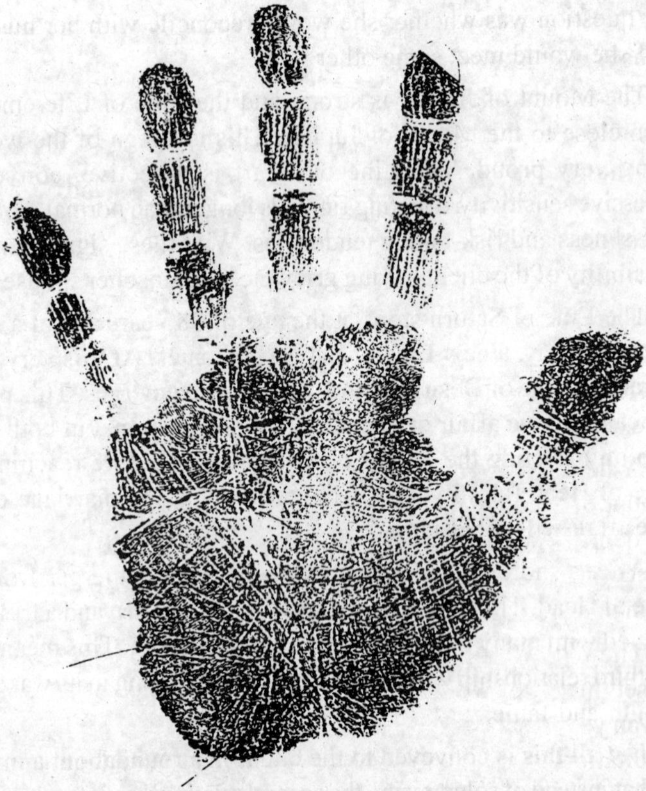

## Handprint 24: Predictions and Remedies

This hand is of a 35-year old woman who wanted to know when she would get married.

The network of lines on the palm indicates the client's nature to remain in a state of dilemma and not take any decisions. The Line of Heart, the Line of Head and the Line of Life arise near the Mount of Jupiter indicate his very proud nature.

The points of emergence for the Line of Life and the Line of Head are not clear. This indicates hurdles in her health but the question by the client does not pertain to her health; it is about her marriage.

The right time for her marriage had come at the age of 28 years when the Line of Mercury emerges from the Line of Life, but marriage had not occurred then. The reason has been cited above — extreme pride and dilemma.

A depression between the ages of 32 to 35 years below the Mount of Sun and the LIne of Head points to obstructions. After the depression, the Line of Mercury emerges before moving in the direction of the Mount of Sun. Hence, there is a possibility of the woman marrying at the age of 35 years.

The reason for this woman's mental turmoil is her pride. To offset this, she is advised to avoid wearing a pukhraj and practice dhyan yoga (meditation) to obtain mental peace (description of the meditation procedure is given in the fourth chapter).

***Handprint No. 25***

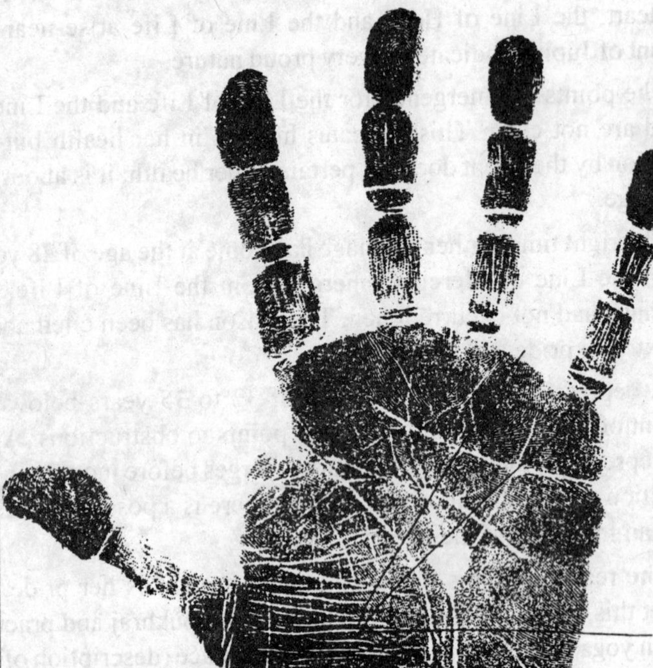

## Handprint 25: Prediction

This hand is of a 36-year old youth, who wanted to leave his service and start a business.

The hand is broad and the fingers are knotted which convey that the person is active and possesses an analytical mind. The lines are not too many, indicating that there are no dilemmas in front of the person. His goal is clear. In the middle of the palm, till the age of 38 years, there is a depression. The Line of Saturn arising before this depression reappears and a new Line of Mercury appears. This is the time for struggle that is nearing its end. Hence it is an appropriate time for setting up a new enterprise. Between 45 to 50 years, the Line of Saturn is somewhat faint but the Line of Mercury is clear, indicating benefits after some time.

Hence, there is no need to get worried on facing problems. At the age of 60, the Line of Obstruction bisects a portion of the Lines of Sun and Saturn but despite the hurdles, the lines do not halt. Subsequently, there is no obstruction. People with broad hands are able to overcome obstacles. Therefore there is no need for taking any remedial measures.

***Handprint No. 26***

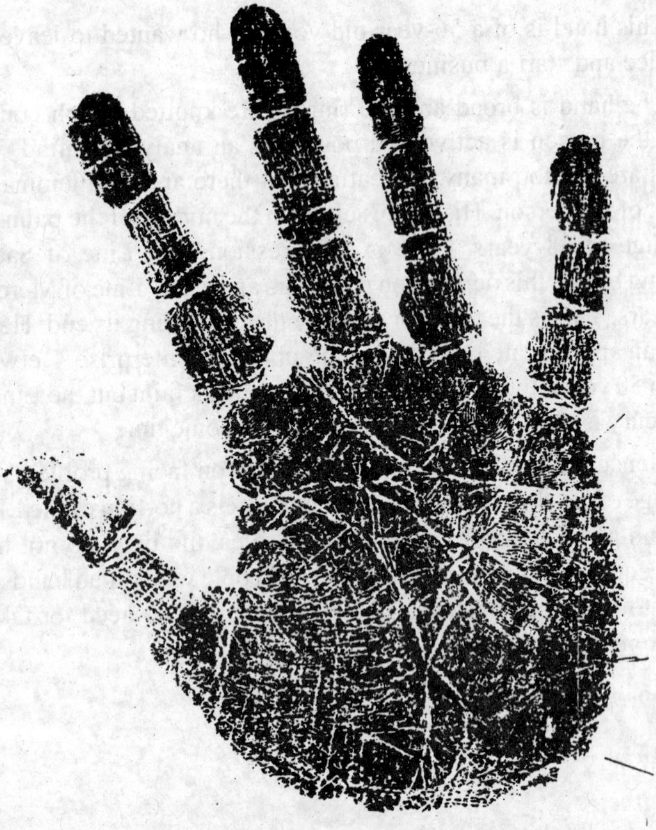

## Handprint 26: Prediction and Remedies

This hand belongs to a 26-year old girl who visited us to ask when she would get married.

The hand is broad and heavy. Her Line of Life emerges attached to the Line of Head. In between the two is an island present till the age of 28 years (according to the gauge of the Line of Life). An island like this at the end of the Line of Life is in the area of Saturn and which, according to the principle of the Line of Saturn and the Line of Mercury, conveys the period of 28 years as suitable for marriage. After this hurdle, a new Line of Mercury is seen arising. Hence there is the possibility of marriage at the age of 28 years.

At 31 years, the Line of Sun emerges. When the Lines of Influence meet at the junction of the Line of Head, a star is formed (at the age of 35 years) on that line. Along with this star, a new branch emerges from the Line of Head. After the star, the Line of Sun breaks into many branches, as a result of which there is a possibility of the client's mental strength decreasing at the age of 35 years.

The client is told not to put too much pressure on her brain and keep getting her eyes tested at regular intervals. She is also advised to pour water every morning in front of the sun and never stare unblinkingly at the sun. She is also told to practice digital postures to strengthen the brain (the procedure for digital postures to strengthen the brain is given in the fourth chapter of this book).

*Handprint No. 27*

## Handprint 27: Prediction and Remedies

This is the hand of a 31-year old Sikh youth working in a government hospital. He wanted to start his own practice by leaving his regular job.

The Line of Saturn (Line of Desire) in the form of a branch of the Line of Life arises at the age of 31 years. Prior to this, the Line of Mercury has emerged from the Line of Life at 28 years, but between 31 and 40 years, the Line of Mercury and the Line of Saturn are very thick. The Line of Sun emanating before 38 years, tilts at one point to reappear clearly from another spot at the age of 35 years.

According to these signs, the answer to the client's query is that time is right for him to leave his service and start his own practice but the period between 31 to 35 years would be full of struggle. The cause for struggle is the presence of many whorls on his fingertips. A person with excessive whorls makes no compromises in front of his own desires. But this is no reason to get troubled as the rest of the lines after 35 years are good.

To overcome his struggles, the client is advised to pray daily to his gurus in this case, so that he gets the strength to adjust. This way, he would develop an attitude of compromise and the effects of the defective lines would be countered.

***Handprint No. 28***

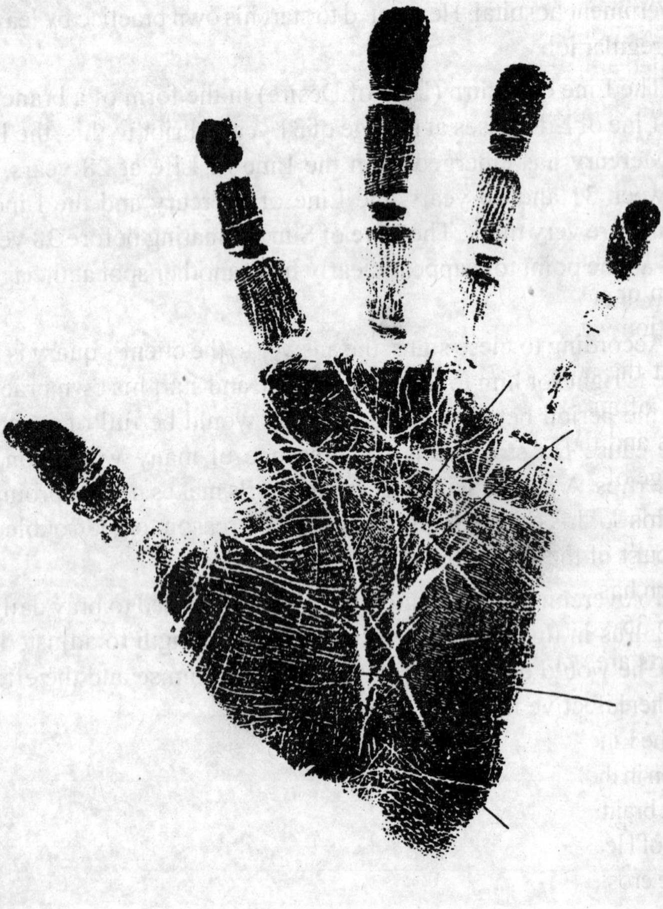

## Handprint 28: Predictions and Remedies

The hand belongs to a 22-year old boy who wanted to go abroad to seek employment. His query was as to when his desire would be fulfilled and what were his chances of getting promotion.

The hand is long and the fingers too are long, indicating the client's tendency to draw up plans and complete each piece of work with refinement. The client is not suitable for work that involves physical labour.

A branch of the Line of Life goes towards the Mount of the Moon or the Luna Mount, indicating a visit abroad. The client's question was as to when he would leave.

At the age of 20 years, the Line of Mercury emerges in the form of an island from the Line of Life. This island ends at 26 years and the Line of Mercury becomes problem-free. Hence, at the age of 26 years there will be foreign travel for him.

This Line of Mercury stops at 31 years, but a new Line of Mercury emanates from a depression. Prior to this, the Line of Saturn has emerged at 31 years. These signs indicate that between 31 to 35 years of age, benefits will accrue but through struggle. Efforts are made to find out the cause for struggle.

There is a gap between the points of emergence of the Line of Head and the Line of Life. This indicates a tendency to do as he wishes. A star is seen in the beginning and the middle of the Line of Head, pointing to a weak brain. There are too many vertical lines above the top mount of the Line of Heart, conveying that after the age of 50 years, the client will be at the cross roads as he will not have a clear goal before him.

To fight against the struggles and overcome the dilemmas, the client is given the following suggestions to adopt:

- Avoid putting too much pressure on his brain.
- Every morning after casting a glance at his hands, he should with his eyes closed pray to God, saying, 'Give me the strength to tolerate and show me the right path.'
- Recite regularly the sankat nivarak mantra to remove the sufferings (the mantra is given in the fourth chapter of this book).

***Handprint No. 29***

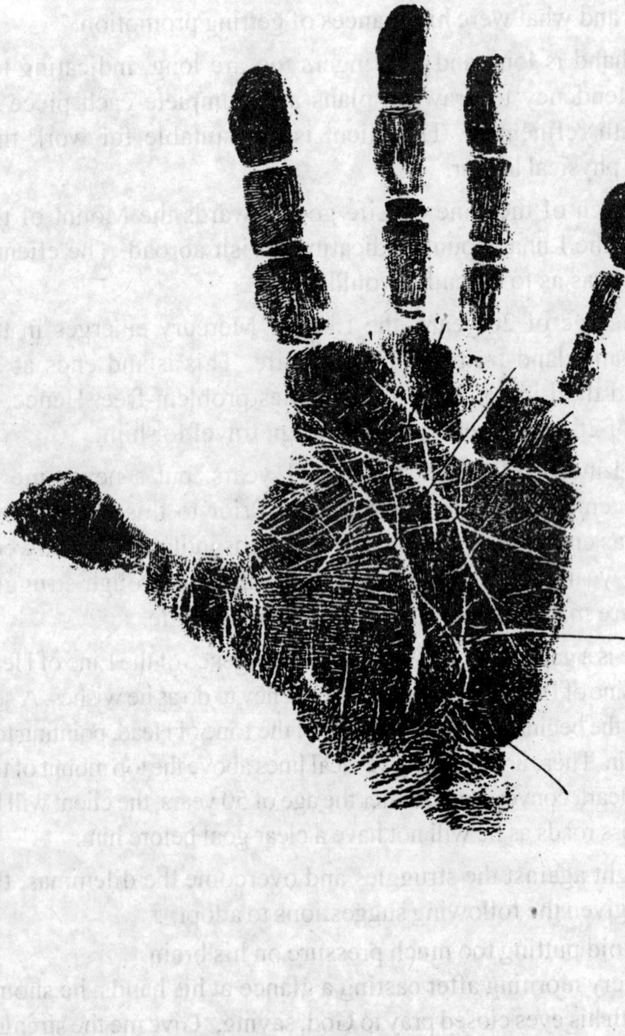

## Handprint 29: Predictions and Remedies

This hand belongs to a 31-year old youth who was an NRI (non-resident Indian). His first marriage had broken and he wanted to know when he would remarry.

A branch of the Line of Life moving towards the Mount of Moon is a sign of foreign residence. At the age of 26 years, the Line of Sun arises and this is the time for his first marriage. This line stops at the age of 31 years, indicating divorce.

Effort is made to identify the cause of divorce. In the fingerprints is seen an excess of whorls and too much distance between the points where the Line of Life and the Line of Head emerge. These signs reveal that in front of his own wish, the client does not listen to anybody. A developed Mount of Jupiter with the presence of a two-branched line conveys excessive pride.

The time for his second marriage is at 36 years, when the Line of Desire emerges from the Line of Life and a new Line of Saturn arises.

This Line of Desire halts at the Line of Head and when the Line of Saturn, moving ahead, turns towards the Mount of Jupiter after 55 years. This line is bisected by lines of obstruction. This reveals that there will be quarrels in the second marriage. To stop these quarrels, he has to wear a ring of iron in his middle finger and stay away from wearing a pukhraj.

***Handprint No. 30***

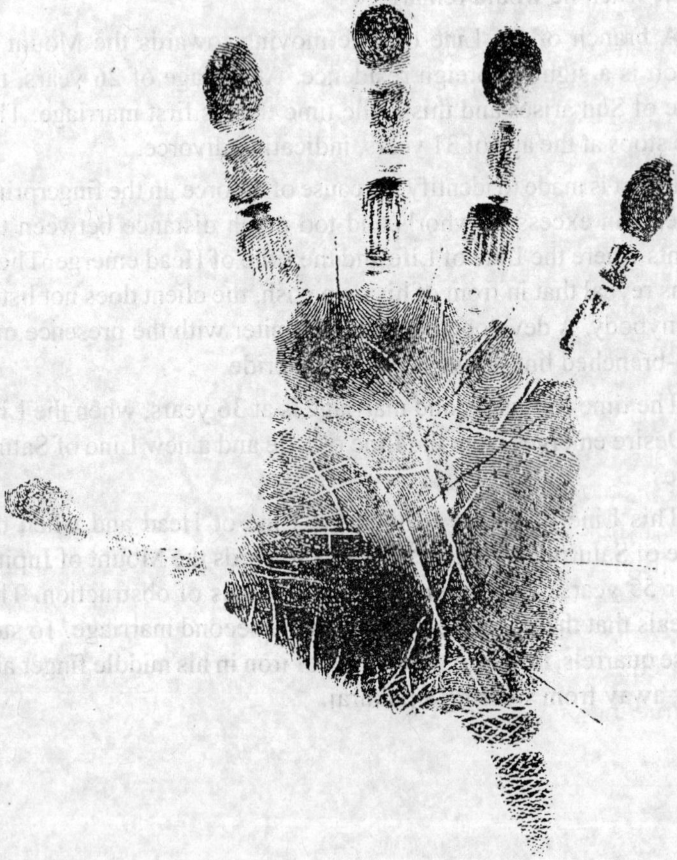

# Handprint 30: Prediction

This hand belongs to an NRI who is 37-years old. His question was when he would get divorce from his wife.

The Line of Life is tilted towards the Mount of Moon or Luna Mount and its branch too moves towards this mount. These signs convey that he is a foreign resident.

There is no Line of Heart on his hand. There is a sole Line of Head that shows that the client lacks in finer sensibilities; he knows only about self-interest.

There is an excess of whorls and the closed loops, revealing the client's tendency to do as he wishes instead of entering into a compromise. Hence divorce will take place, but when?

To get an answer to this question, the position of the Line of Saturn is studied. This line is thick between the ages of 30 to 40 years and at the age of 34 years, another parallel line emanates. This too is faulty. At the age of 40, a line of obstruction arising near the Line of Life goes and intersects the Line of Saturn. After this, there is no line of obstruction on the Line of Saturn. This means that from 30 to 40 years, the period is one of struggle or litigation. The Line of Obstruction ends at the age of 40 years showing that the client will obtain divorce.

The client had no desire to find out the remedies to overcome the obstructions, hence it was futile to tell him anything more.

### Handprint No. 31

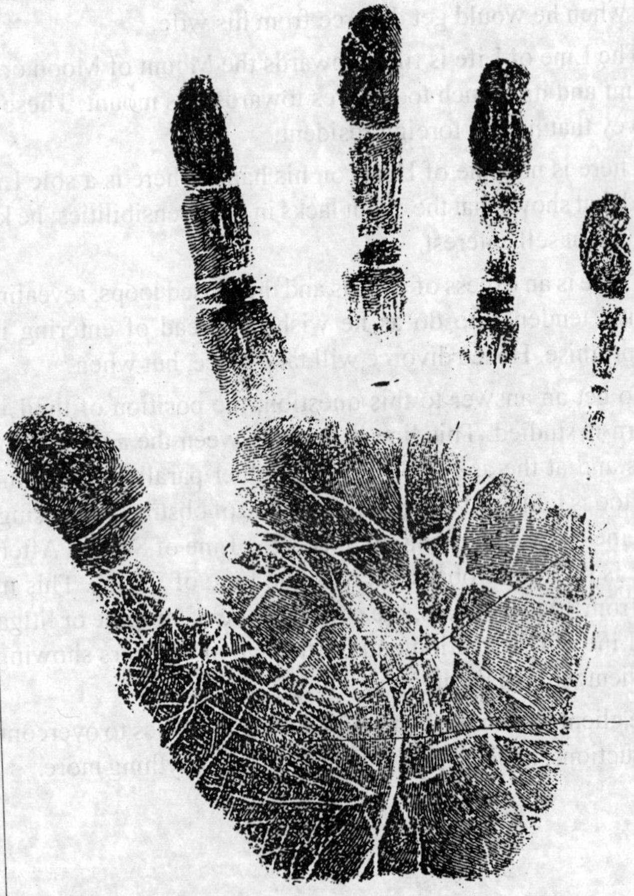

## Handprint 31: Prediction and Remedies

This hand belongs to a 30-year old zamindar (landlord) who made good earnings from farming. He wanted to enter politics and so desired to know which period would be suitable to do so.

The Line of Mercury emerges from the Mount of Moon to reach the Mount of Mercury. In between it gets lost at places. The Line of Mercury is bisected by a Line of Obstruction at the age of 28 years, but by now it was too late. At the age of 30, a new Line of Saturn arises and a parallel Line of Desire emerges from the Line of Life. This is the time to enter politics but at the age of 32 years, a thick Line of Sun is seen emerging. In the Line of Sun and at the junction of the Line of Heart, there is a star. Above the star there is an island near the Mount of Sun.

According to these signs, the period between 32 to 38 years is one of considerable struggle and the age of 50 years is unfavourable for the eyes and the heart. After this, there is the possibility of him earning a bad name.

The client is advised to plunge into politics immediately and wear a topaz ring in his index finger. With this he would acquire the right knowledge that will keep him away from disgrace. He has to recite daily the sankat nivarak mantra for removal of obstacles, as it would help in decreasing the problems (the sankat nivarak mantra is given in the fourth chapter of this book).

***Handprint No. 32***

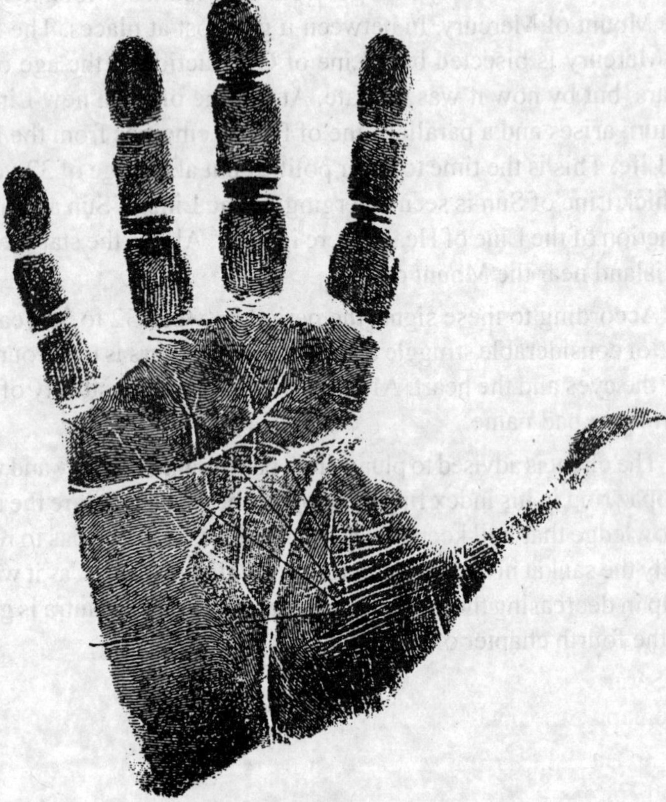

## Handprint 32: Predictions and Remedies

This hand belongs to a 21-year old Muslim boy who wanted to go abroad in search of employment. His query was as to when he would be able to do so.

The Line of Life moves towards the Mount of Moon indicating the possibility of his settling abroad. When? To find an answer to this question, let us look at the positions of the Line of Mercury and the Line of Saturn.

The Line of Mercury arises from within the Line of Life at the age of 18 years. On crossing the Line of Life and on complementing of the Line of Life with the Line of Mercury, an island is formed by the Axe Line between the age of 23 and 28 years. Another island at the same age is seen between the Line of Life and the Line of Head. At the age of 28 years, the Line of Mercury arises clearly and from the same Line of Mercury, a beautiful Line of Saturn emerges at 30 years of age. This means that the time for foreign travel is in the 28the year and promotion will come at 30 years.

The Line of Life, the Line of Head and the Line of Heart are thick, signifying the possibility of promotion but after a period of struggle. Between the age of 38 and 50 years, there are many crosses between the Line of Heart and the Line of Head, indicating a period of problems.

In the upper part of the Line of Heart, there is a beautiful Line of Saturn and the Line of Sun; thus old age will be passed in peace and happiness.

To find relief from problems, the client is advised to pray to his God for mercy and practice tratak on the middle portion of the hand (the procedure for tratak is given in the fourth chapter of this book).

***Handprint No. 33***

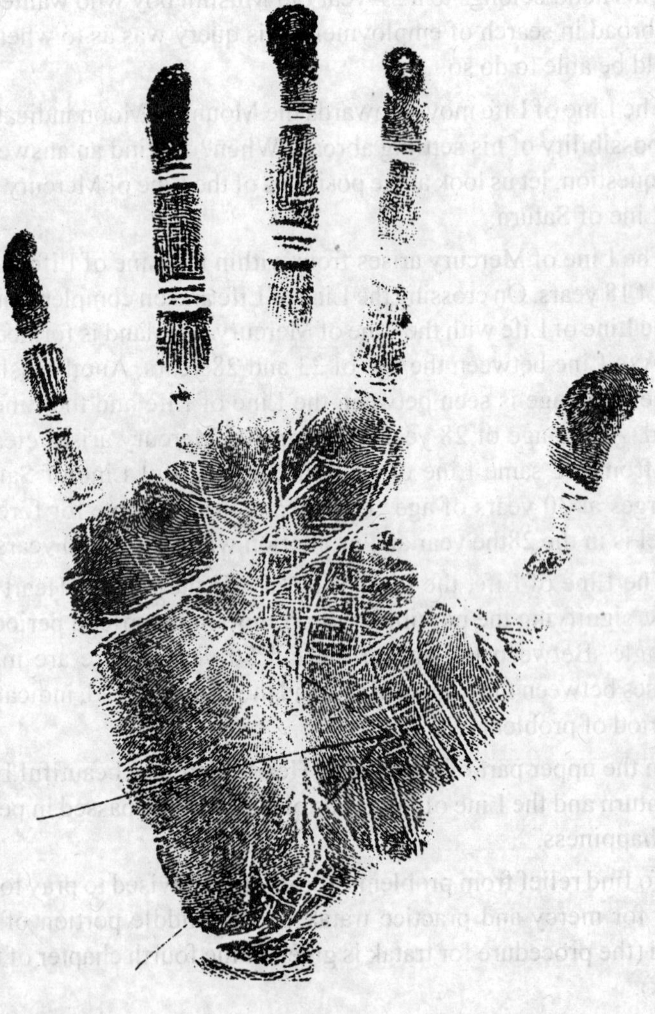

## Handprint 33: Prediction and Remedies

This hand belongs to a 27-year old boy, who wanted to expand his family business. He came to ask what was the right time for doing so.

The palm is long while the fingers are long and knotted. The Line of Heart is defective and in addition, there is a broken Girdle of Venus. Lines of Obstruction cut across the other lines. All these signs convey that the client is adept in chalking out plans but sloppy in executing them. His speed of work is slow. He becomes tense in no time. Such a man gets disappointed at even minor failures. The auspicious sign on this hand is the Line of Head. The Line of Saturn is joined to the Line of Life till the age of 32. After 32 years, a Line of Influence emerging from the Defensive Mars meets the Line of Saturn. Hence, the time for expanding his business is at 32 years of age. At this age, two Lines of Desire arise but the Axe Lines and Lines of Obstruction indicate progress after a period of struggle.

The client is advised that till the age of 32 years, he should chalk out complete plans for his business and subsequently go in for expansion. He is also told to practice anguli mudra (digital postures) for removal of the faults in his Line of Heart and for strengthening the heart. In addition, he has to practice dhyan yoga (mediation) every day to remain free from tension (see the steps for both these postures in the fourth chapter of this book).

On wearing an emerald ring in the little finger, his behaviour towards others would improve and by wearing a coral ring in his ring finer, his ability to work hard would increase. This is a palm where the influence of Saturn predominates, hence it is inadvisable for him to wear a blue sapphire or iron ring. His index finger is longer than normal and the Mount of Jupiter is well developed; hence pukhraj is to be avoided.

***Handprint No. 34***

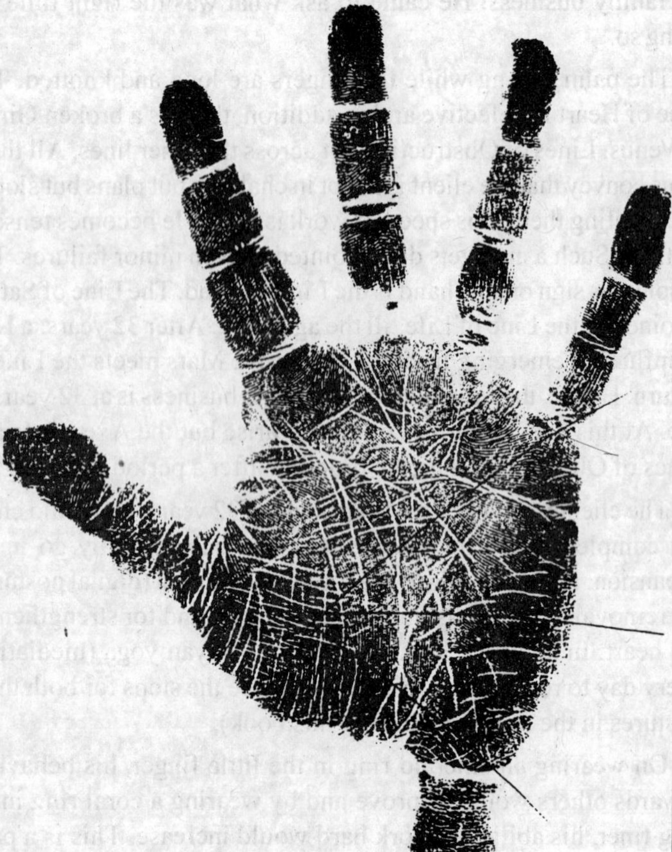

## Handprint 34: Prediction and Remedies

This hand belongs to a 25-year old youth who wanted to enter politics while his parents wanted him to join M.BA. Caught in a dilemma, this youth visited our Institute to show his palm and find out the right path to take.

The palm is broad and heavy. The fingers are thick. The Line of Life, the Line of Mars and the Line of Saturn are so intermingled that it is difficult to locate the Line of Life among them. The Line of Head is short. These signs reveal his inability to be successful in M.BA., so the other field left with him is politics which also happens to be the client's desire.

The incomplete Line of Life with its branch meets the Line of Saturn to complete its further journey. Till the age of 33 years, the Line of Life and the Line of Mars continue as one line. The Line of Mars that is longer than the Line of Life provides support to the Line of Life.

After his studies, the other alternative left for the client is to enter politics. The Line of Mercury emerges from the two-in-one Line of Life at the age of 24 years. Prior to this, a Line of Saturn has emerged at the age of 27 years. A Line of Obstruction crosses the Line of Saturn at 27 years. Hence dilemma and hurdles plague him till 27 years of age, after which he can enter fully into politics.

The time for emergence of the Line of Saturn from the two-in-one Line of Life is 33 years. This desire occupies the form of a line. At the age of 35, a new Line of Sun arises. The subsequent lines, making squares and triangles, move towards the fingers. The significance of all this is that the client may enter politics at the age of 27 years but he would gain recognition only at 33 years. To make the period, prior to this, favourable, the client is advised to wear a ring of iron in his middle finger. Persons with broad and heavy palms are dominated by Mars, hence coral is not permissible for them.

## *Handprint No. 35*

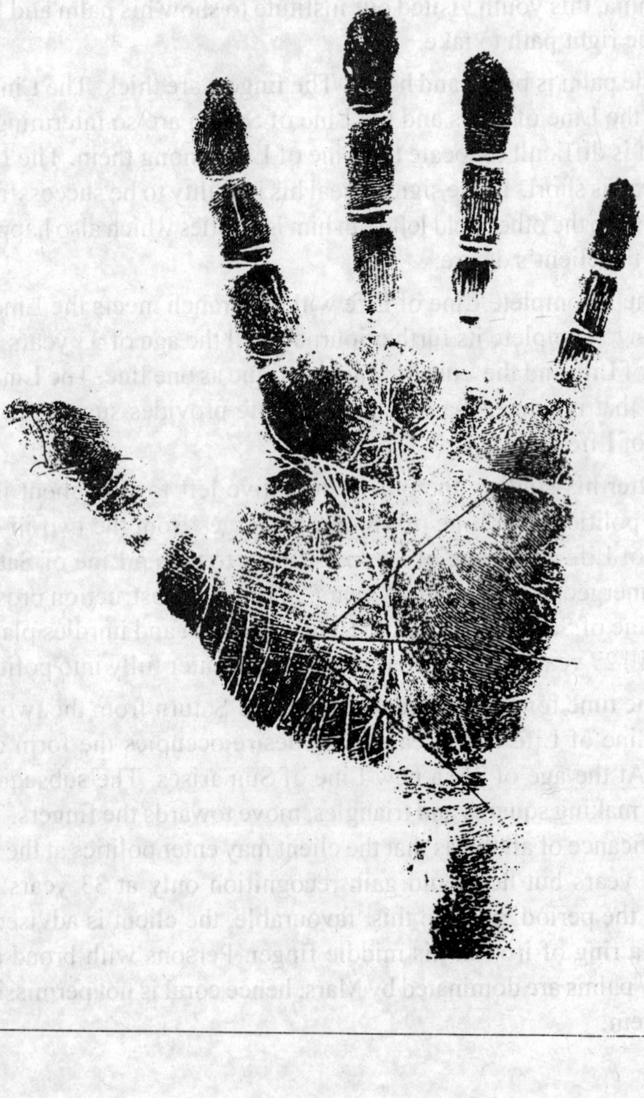

## Handprint 35: Prediction and Remedies

This hand is of a 49-year old man whose father had married three times. This client was the offspring from the first wife. Four children were born from the other two step-mothers. The father had not bothered about his children and it was the client who had brought up his step-brothers and step-sisters, but not even one of them was grateful to him. As a result, the client was mentally upset and his query was as to when he would find happiness.

In this palm, most of the lines emerge from the inner side of the Line of Life, conveying primacy of familial responsibilities. The Line of Heart is thick, indicating tension.

The Line of Saturn and the Line of Mercury are good, conveying a sound financial position. The Line of Heart is thick which indicates a severe blow to his sentiments. All the lines above the Line of Heart and moving near the fingers are devoid of hurdles; hence the period after 55 years will be peaceful.

To make the troublesome period peaceful till this age, the client is advised to practice anguli mudra (digital postures) to make the heart strong. He is also an ardent believer in Sai Baba, so he is told to take keen interest in Sai Baba's kirtans (prayers) and lead a life keeping in mind the motto: 'Do your duty without expecting any reward.'

*Handprint No. 36*

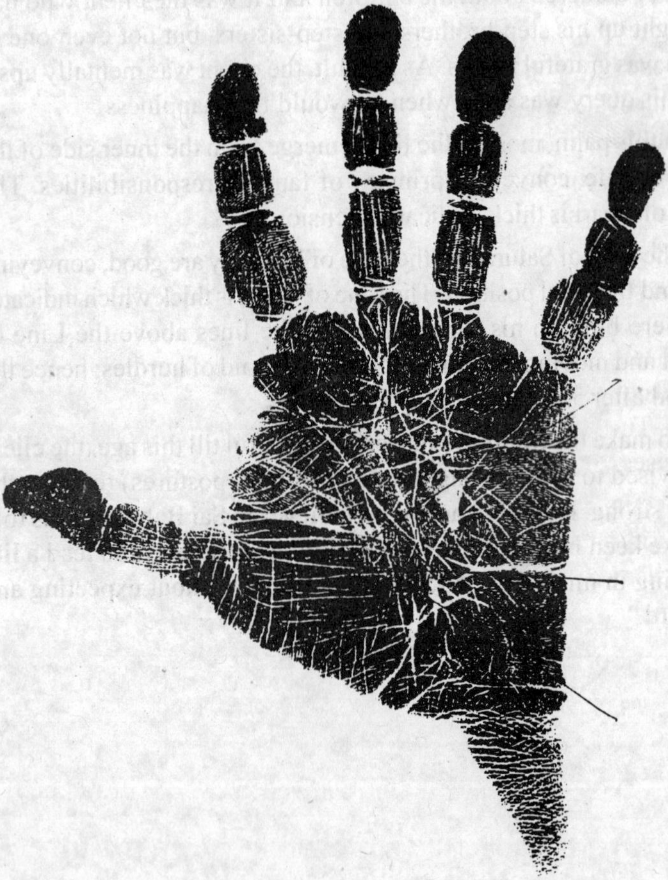

## Handprint 36: Prediction and Remedies

This is the hand of a 32-year old youth who had been married for eight years but had no child. His query was as to when he would become a father.

The Line of Life is straight and by joining the Line of Saturn, it completes its journey. The Line of Mars is long but a star is present at the end of the line, signifying obstruction. As a star is present in the centre of the Mount of Moon, it indicates some form of loss in the central portion of the body. A Line of Division between the palm and the base of the thumb shows faint islands.

The line above the bracelet lines stands upright like a bow pointing upwards. These signs are hurdles in the birth of progeny but the most useful sign among them is that at the base of the thumb, on the Mount of Venus, three lines indicating progeny are clearly visible. This means that after removal of the hurdles, a child will be born. To find out the duration of the hurdle, take a look below the Mount of Sun. The depression will end at 40 years, after which the Line of Sun arises.

To counter the hurdles, the spiritual path is to recite the mantra for bearing a child and to consult a medical specialist for removal of physical defects (see the Santan Gopal mantra for the birth of a child in the fourth chapter of this book).

***Handprint No. 37***

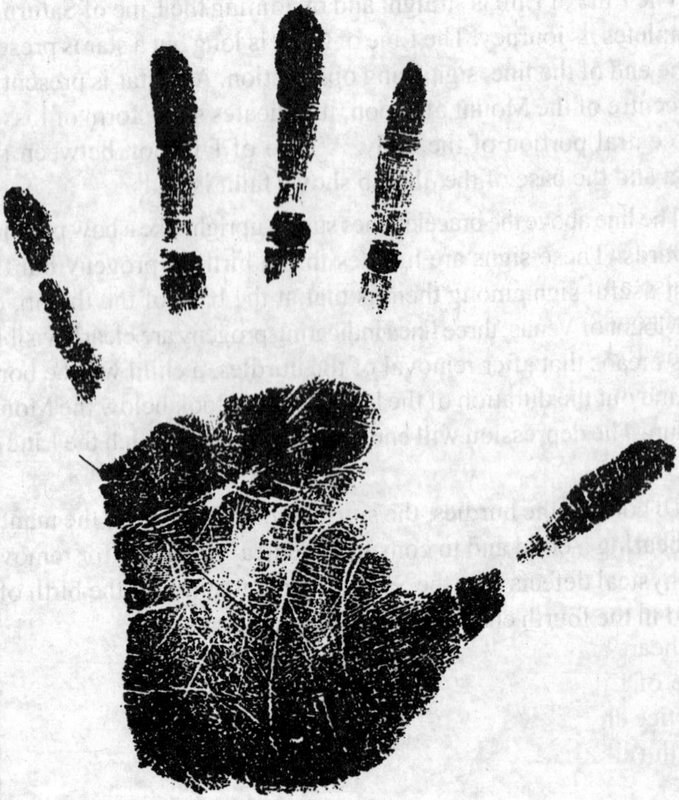

## Handprint 37: Prediction and Remedies

This hand belongs to a 25-year old girl who wanted to join the electronic media and came to find out when she would be successful in it.

The hand is long and so are her fingers. Both these signs indicate that the client has the capability to draw up plans and it is in her nature to delve deep into every task that she undertakes. Hence, a career in the electronic media is suitable for her.

But with our inquisitive readers we want to discuss the signs which will provide the answers to questions which the client has not asked. The signs are the islands on the Line of Life and on the Line of Mars. An unusually long Line of Heart endowed with islands as also a broken Line of Head with a depression in its centre are not a good sign. A large gap exists between the points of emergence of the Line of Life and the Line of Head. All these signs indicate the client's sensitiveness and nature to do according to her strong will. Because of these signs, we predict tension and blow to her ego.

Instead of revealing all these details to the client, she is told, "Your extreme sensitiveness keeps you tense and this will cast an adverse impact on your health." To escape from all this, she is advised to practice anguli mudra (digital postures) for strengthening the heart and those for strengthening the Line of Head and the Line of Life. To remain free of tension, she is told to regularly practice dhyan yoga or meditation, as it would be beneficial for her health (all these postures are given in the fourth chapter of this book).

### *Handprint No. 38*

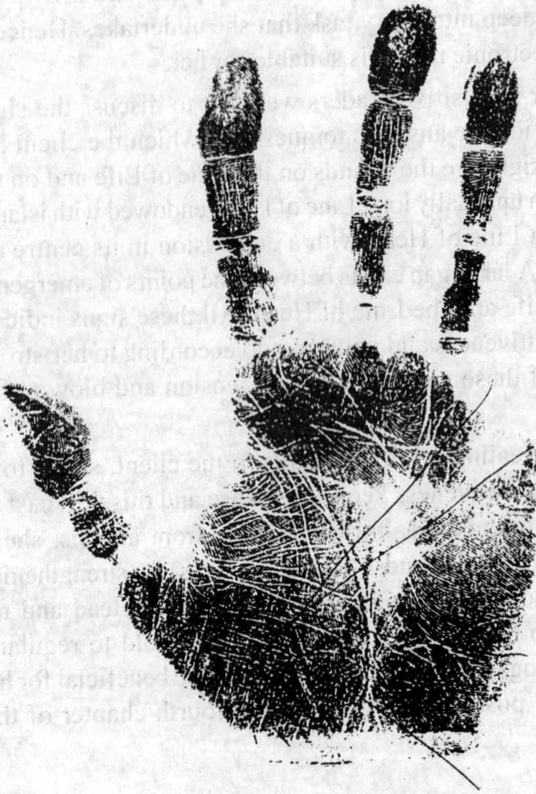

## Handprint 38: Prediction and Remedies

This is the hand of a 40-year old youth who worked abroad in a travel agency. His duty entailed travelling to other countries because of which he got very little time to spend with his wife. He wanted to know about his future.

The Line of Life is thick and the Line of Saturn (Line of Desire) emerging from it is thick too. There is a depression parallel to this Line of Desire and this casts its impact till the age of 45 years. Between the Line of Head and the Line of Heart is a bridge-like line and the Line of Heart is fragmented. All these signs reveal a life of struggle and shocks to the heart.

The auspicious signs on this palm are the vertical lines on the Mount of Sun and the trident on the Line of Saturn. Their effect is seen after the age of 50 years. To make the period till this age trouble-free, the client is advised to practice dhyan yoga (meditation) while his wife is asked to daily recite the Gayatri mantra on a string or mala of beads. Refer to the method of meditation and Gayatri mantra in the fourth chapter of this book.

*Chapter 3*

# A Comparative Study of 12 Case Histories

## Introduction

In the book, 'Palmistry, How to Master It', published by this Institute, three handprints of the same person, from youth to old age, have been printed to prove that there is a possibility of the hand lines undergoing a change. The reason for this change is the change in the mental state of the person.

In this chapter the fact that changes in the lines do occur was confirmed by keeping in front of each other the handprints of a man taken during childhood and during his youth. Handprint 39 of the client has been taken at the age of nine years and handprint 40 of the same client was taken at the age of 25 years. On studying the differences between the two, you will learn that with changes in the mental state, changes take place in one's destiny too.

In this chapter, some handprints of different members of the same family are given. At one time they had come together to the Institute, and later some of them visited us separately with different types of questions on different days.

To answer questions pertaining to children, it is advisable to see the palms of both the husband and wife. The handprints of one such childless couple are given in this chapter. It is hoped that this comparative study will prove beneficial for those interested in acquiring knowledge of palmistry.

***Handprint No. 39***
***Age 9 Years***

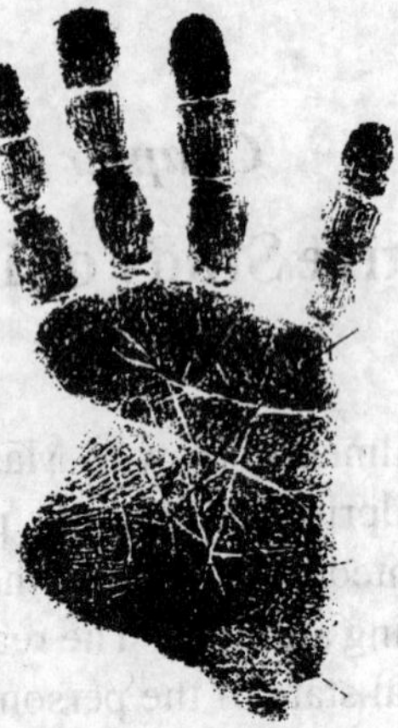

***Handprint No. 40***
***Age 25 Years***

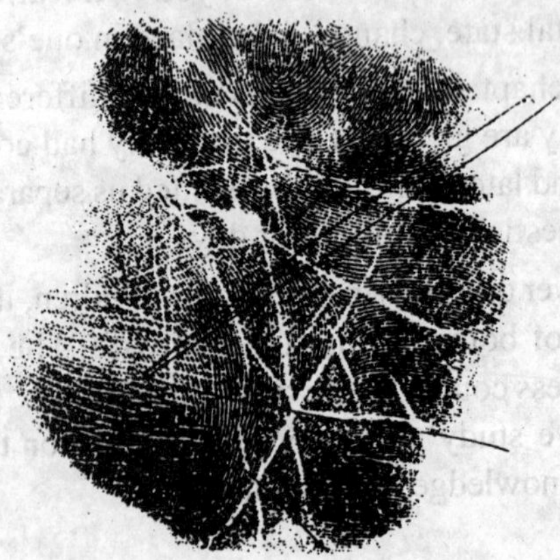

## Handprints 39 and 40: A Comparative Study

Handprint 39 belongs to a client during childhood and handprint 40 is of the same client at the time of his youth.

The Line of Life in the handprint of childhood is incomplete. Its one branch joins the Line of Saturn to complete its length. This Line of Life indicates serious family problems at 40 years. In the handprint taken during youth, this Line of Life is faint but it becomes clear later on to reach the wrist. This shows the possibility of his troubles lessening.

The Line of Head is long but, in the handprint taken during childhood, there is a faint depression in the middle of this line. According to the Line of Saturn, this depression signifies mental tension at 40 years of age. After this depression, the Line of Saturn halts at 45 years. This means that there is a change in employment after the mental tension gets over. The parallel line signifies a separate source of income. Subsequently the Line of Saturn halts beyond 50 years.

The Line of Mercury is present in both the handprints, right from childhood to old age, but after the age of 28 years, the triangle next to the Line of Mercury is incomplete in the handprint of childhood. In the handprint of youth, it becomes complete, indicating positive gains between 28 to 35 years. A branch is seen emerging from the Line of Saturn at the age of 32 years to move along the Line of Mercury till 40 years. The branch is absent in the handprint of childhood and there are many fragmented lines on the Mount of Sun, above the Line of Heart. In the handprint of youth, there is a clear vertical line on the Mount of Sun. In other words, in comparison to the print of childhood, there has been an improvement in the handprint of youth.

***Handprint No. 41***
***Hand of Husband***

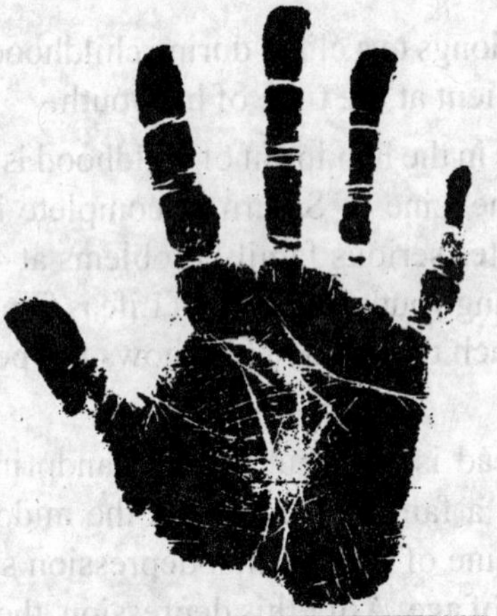

***Handprint No. 42***
***Hand of Wife***

## Handprints 41 and 42: Predictions

Both these handprints belong to an NRI couple settled in Britain (UK). Handprint 41 is of a 63-year old husband and handprint 42 is that of his 62-year old wife. Branches of the Line of Life on both the hands are seen moving towards the Mount of Moon or the Luna Mount, confirming their foreign residence. The thick lines on both the hands indicate the story of their life of struggle.

The husband had started a pub in London. He invested a major share of his earnings in shares but faced severe losses. The thick Axe Line running parallel to the Line of Mercury indicates losses and the initial portion of the Line of Head reveals an incomplete island.

The wife's health is not good as is evident from the vertical and horizontal lines on the Mount of Moon. The cause of her poor health is tension and the reason for tension is the distance between the points where the Line of Life and the Line of Head emerge. In other words, the wife has the tendency to dominate but in front of her husband, she is unable to have her way. As a result, tension arises and upsets the equilibrium of her body, thus affecting her health.

Both of them receive old age pension (social security) from the government on account of being senior citizens. Hence, their old age will be a period of happiness. These signs are visible on both the palms.

In the palms of both the man and his wife, vertical lines on the mounts above the Line of Heart are obstacle-free during old age. During their tour of India, they had paid a visit to the Institute when we had taken their handprints.

***Handprint No. 43***
***Elder Brother 26 Years***

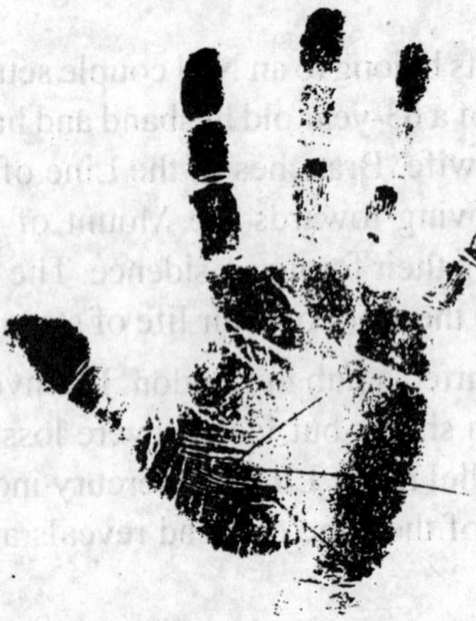

***Handprint No. 44***
***Younger Brother 23 Years***

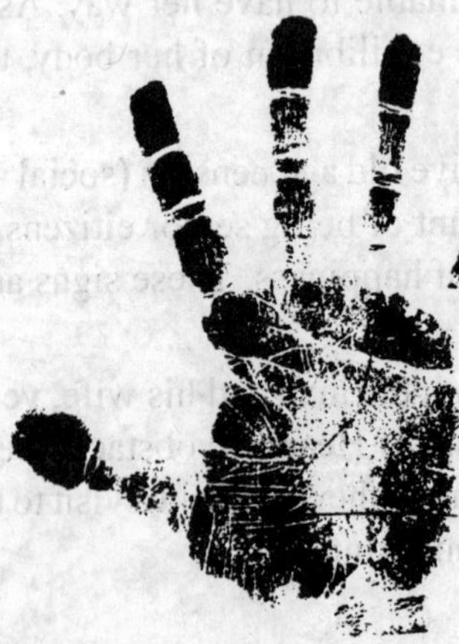

## Handprints 43 and 44: Predictions

Both these palms belong to two brothers. Both were engaged in a battle over the division of their property. Both of them came at separate timings to show their palms at the Institute.

The distance between the points of beginning of the Line of Life and the Line of Head on the palms of both the brothers indicates a genetic tendency of having their own way.

The main lines of the older brother are thick and islands are seen on the Line of Mercury from childhood till the age of 30 years. Subsequently, the line becomes thick and faint. The area below the Mount of Sun is depressed. The Line of Life has no supportive line to it.

The ring finger of the younger brother is longer than normal, indicating a tendency to take risks. The little finger is longer than normal, pointing to an excessively cunning nature. The Line of Heart is thick, indicating blows to his sensitivities. The Line of Life after 35 years is made of islands that point to family troubles, though the Line of Saturn and the Line of Sun are good. This shows that it would not be harmful for him to take some risks. Thus the younger brother is advised to wear an iron ring in his middle finger and a pukhraj ring in his index finger, so that his cunning nature is kept in check and he is prevented from indulging in corruption.

The Line of Desire emerges from the Line of Life of the younger brother at the age of 35 years but subsequently this line becomes full of islands, showing that from the viewpoint of family life, the period after 35 years is bad. From the financial point of view, the elder brother's life is worse in comparison to the younger one's. He is advised to recite the sankat nivaran mantra for overcoming his problems (see this mantra in the fourth chapter of this book).

***Handprint No. 45***
***Husband 35 Years***

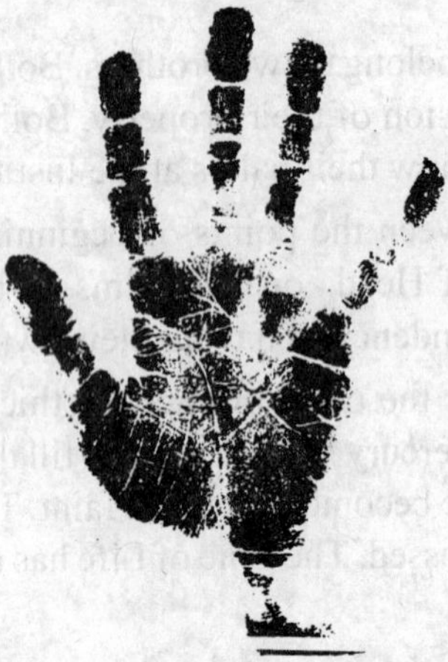

***Handprint No. 46***
***Wife 30 Years***

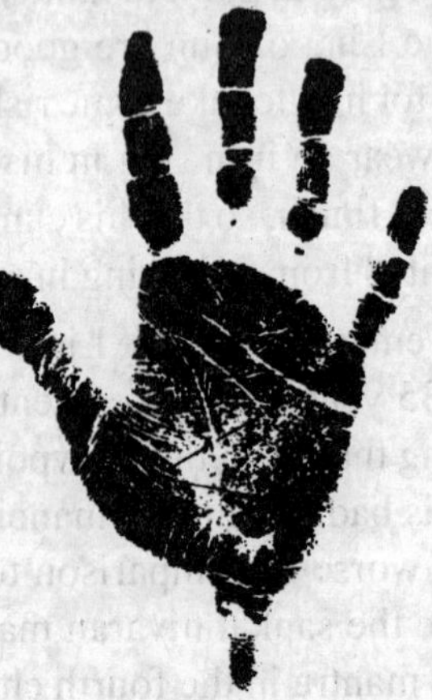

## Handprints 45 and 46: Predictions

Both these hands belong to a husband and wife. Both were desperate to have a child.

The Lines of Division in both their hands at the base of their thumbs are fragmented, pointing to difficulties in having a child. However, after the Line of Division, the wife has many lines showing children. Her husband has two lines for children. This shows that both are fertile, but they have to encounter hurdles in giving birth to a child.

At the age of 36 years, a Line of Desire emerges from the Line of Life on the wife's palm, while at the age of 42 years, the Line of Desire emanates from the Life Line on the husband's palm. As per their query, this is an opportune time for bearing a child.

The couple is advised to undergo a medical checkup so as to overcome the physical hurdles and daily recite the Santan Gopal mantra (mantra for bearing a child) to enhance their spiritual strength (see this mantra in the fourth chapter of this book). In the husband's palm, there are other signs of obstruction, like islands, which are related to wealth, etc., but these do not fall in the purview of the question asked.

***Handprint No. 47***
***Husband 40 Years***

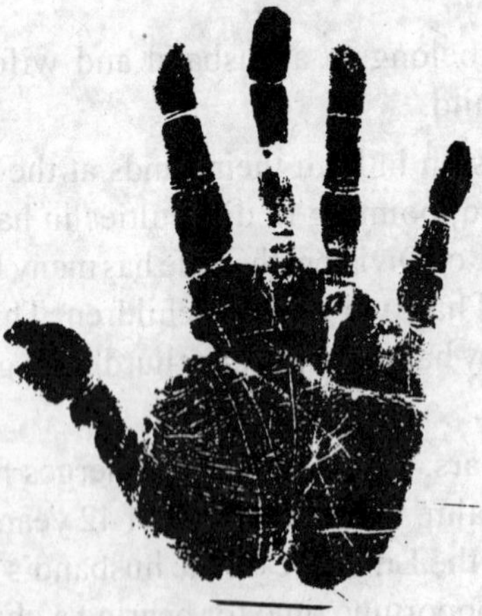

***Handprint No. 48***
***Wife 38 Years***

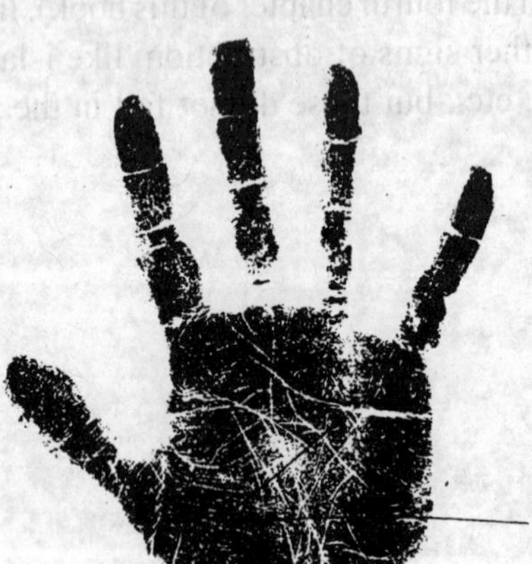

## Handprints 47 and 48: Predictions

Both these handprints belong to a couple that strongly desires to give birth to a child. The Line of Life of the husband is incomplete but gets completed by the Line of Saturn. The defects in the Line of Life are countered by a beautiful Line of Mars. The wife's Line of Mars and the Line of Life are incomplete and fragmented. All these indicate hurdles.

The Line of Division dividing the thumbs of both the husband and wife from the Mount of Venus is fragmented and this is obstructing the birth of progeny. The wife has a single line for a child, but it is short. Both of them had tried all kinds of medical treatments but their desire remained unfulfilled.

Both were advised to recite the mantra for the birth of a child and observe a fast on the day of Bhishma Ashtami. If after a period of three years, no fruitful results were obtained, then they were advised to adopt an orphan.

***Handprint No. 49***
***Husband 37 Years***

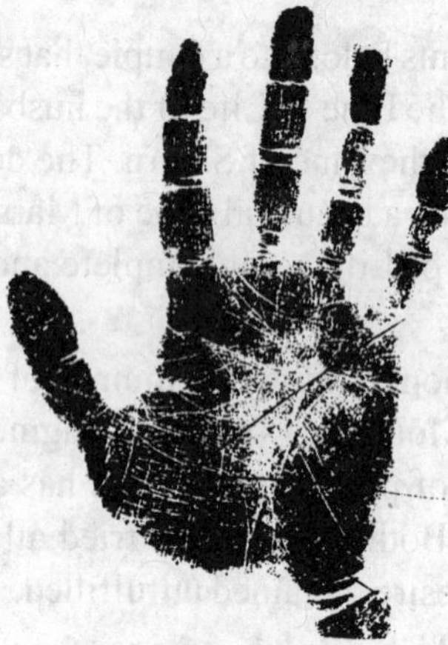

***Handprint No. 50***
***Wife 32 Years***

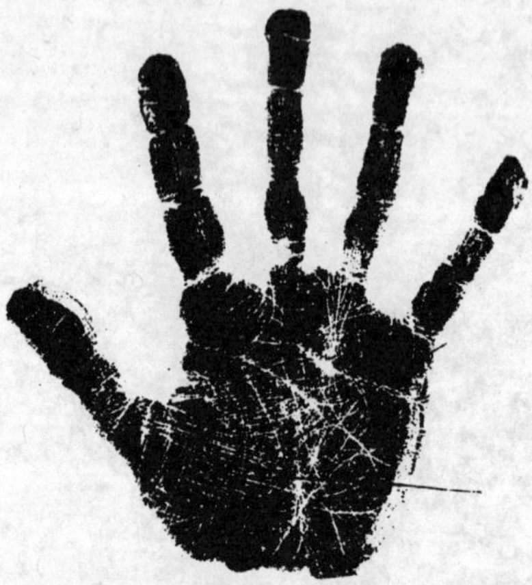

## Handprints 49 and 50: Predictions

Both these handprints belong to a husband and wife. At different intervals, both of them had come to the Institute to show their palms. Both were unhappy with each other. Not that they wanted divorce, but both longed for happiness.

The Lines of Sexuality in both the hands are incltilted towards the Heart Line and are fragmented, pointing to marital problems.

There are networks of lines in both the hands and these are criss-crossed by all kinds of signs and symbols. These indicate a life of tension. In both the hands, the Line of Heart, the Line of Head and the branches of the Girdle of Venus are seen merging into each other. These signify that decisions in life are taken by the couple with their hearts and not their brains.

On the wife's Mount of Jupiter, many rings of Jupiter are present that express her desire to receive respect but which is left unfulfilled, adding to her tension. The Line of Head on the husband's palm is short, indicating lack of mental strength. Such an unmatched couple is suggested the following measures to adopt:

- Both of them should practice dhyan yoga (meditation).
- The husband should practice the anguli mudra (digital postures) to strengthen the brain while the wife is advised to perform digital postures that strengthen her heart.
- The wife is asked to recite the Gauri mantra daily, while the husband is told to recite the Shiv mantra.
- The wife should refrain from wearing a phukraj. (see these remedies in the fourth chapter of this book).

*Chapter 4*

# Remedies for Removal of Obstacles

## Introduction

A person who approaches an astrologer or a palmist is either facing some problem or is caught in a dilemma. The duty of a well-wishing palmist is to suggest the remedies for solving the problems of the person, so that the person can free himself/herself from tension. Further, the trouble-torn person is advised to take the path that suits his basic nature as it will prove beneficial in getting rid of his dilemma. Hence, in the books published by this Institute, remedies to remove hurdles have been provided. In the Institute's book entitled, 'A Handbook of Scientific and Practical Palmistry', we have thrown light upon the scientific aspects of the remedies to improve one's future.

In this chapter we are providing the descriptions of only those remedies that have been referred to in the second and third chapters of the book. Here we consider it essential to add that for the remedies to prove effective, faith also plays a major role. Such remedies should be told that suit the religion and mental attitude of the client, else full benefits will not accrue.

**Easy Steps to: Dhyan Yoga (Meditation)**

Close your eyes and breathe in slowly and gradually through the nose while uttering in the mind, "I am breathing in." Immediately afterwards, breathe out slowly through the nose and repeat within your heart, "I am breathing out."

This exercise of breathing in and breathing out should be repeated for 10 minutes. This way, the mind calms down and relief is obtained from all tensions and the strength to still the mind (meditate) is enhanced.

The difference between this meditation and pranayama is that the breath is held within, both when breathing in and breathing out, whereas in dhyan yoga (meditation), one has to experience the entry and exit of the breaths.

**Tratak Vidhi (the Procedure of Staring)**

Staring at an object or any part of the body without blinking the eyes is known as tratak. Ordinarily the eyelids flutter at each and every moment. The act of preventing the eyelids from fluttering for a minute, or half a minute or one-fourth of minute is known as tratak. One should not stare or do tratak for more than a minute.

**Anguli Mudra**

***Digital Postures for Strengthening the Brain***

These postures are executed by touching the tip of the index finger to the tip of the thumb. Even if the Line of Head is defective or the Mount of Jupiter is extra developed or underdeveloped, benefit is derived from this posture. Practise this posture daily every morning and every evening for 15 minutes each.

***Digital Postures for Increasing Vitality***

This posture or mudra is executed by touching the fingertip of the little finger and the ring finger together to the tip of the thumb. With this, the defects in the Line of Life and the Line of Mercury are removed. If the Mount of Venus or Mount of Aggressive Mars is underdeveloped, then practice this mudra daily for 15 minutes every morning and evening.

***Digital Postures for Relieving Defects of Saturn***

This mudra is formed when the index finger is bent to touch its tip to the Mont of Venus, while keeping the other fingers and the thumb separate. If the Mount of Saturn or the Line of Saturn is defective, then by doing this mudra, benefit is gained. Practise this mudra every morning and evening for 15 minutes each.

Saturn-dominated persons are more prone to developing orthopaedic and vata-related problems. This mudra proves effective in treating *vata*-related diseases.

***Digital Postures for Strengthening Heart***

This posture or mudra is done when, with the exception of the little finger, the tips of the other three fingers touch the tip of the thumb. If the Line of Heart is defective or the Mount of Sun is extra developed, then such a person can acquire benefit from this mudra.

Those persons who suffer from high blood pressure or heart problems or who have had a stroke, they should daily practice this mudra or posture. Benefit will accrue by daily practice of this mudra every morning and evening. If the client is on medicinal treatment, then he should not stop taking the medicines prescribed.

**Mantra to Remove Obstacles**

***Sankat Nivarak Mantra***

*Om namah Ganeshaye* .

To find relief from problems like debt, litigation, etc., regularly recite the mantra on the string of beads or mala and observe a fast on every Ganesh Chaturthi day.

***Sarva Sukh Karak Gayatri Mantra***

*Om bhurbhuvah swaha*

*Tat saviturvaraynyam.*

*Bhargo devasya dhimahi,*

*dhiyo yo naha prachodyat*

***Gauri Mantra for Removal of Hurdles in a Girl's Marriage***

*Katyayani mahamaye*

*Maha yoginyadhishwari.*

*Nanda gop sutam devi*

*Patime kurute namah*

***Shiva Mantra***

*Om namah Shivaye*

***Santan Gopal Mantra***

*Om shri hrin klin glon Devaki sutaan Govinda Vasudeva jagatpate*

*Dehi may tanayam Krishna twamhamam sharanam gatah*

Recite this mantra every morning. A husband and wife who desire to give birth to a child should pray to God on the Saptami of Bhadra Paksh Shukla and regularly observe a fast.

Those who have a girl child and do not practice family planning in the hope of giving birth to a son next time, they should consider every girl as a gift from God. To bear a male child, they should every year make donations on the day of Bhishmashtami. This way the inability to bear a son to light your pyre is countered and no need is felt for performing the shraddha (a ceremony in honour of the *Pitara* dead relations). Every year in the month of Magha on the Shuklapaksh day, Bhishmashtami should be celebrated.

**For Removal of Hurdles**

***Use of Gems in Rings***

Every finger and every mount on the hand is attached to the brain through the nerves. Hence, after seeing the developed or underdeveloped state of the mount, we give advice on which gem to wear.

The length and thickness of the finger is taken into account when advising on the gem to wear. On wearing a ring with a gem encased in it on the particular finger, a special centre of the brain is activated, bringing a change in the person's disposition. A ring worn with this objective should be open at the base so that the finger stays in contact with the gem.

If the Mount of Jupiter is underdeveloped or the index finger is shorter than normal, then a ring of pukhraj or yellow sapphire should be worn in the index finger. The Mount of Saturn is normally depressed. If the middle finger is longer than normal, then the Mount of Saturn is considered developed. When the middle finger is smaller than normal, then a ring of iron should be worn in the middle finger.

To remove the defects of Saturn, a blue sapphire is advisable but at times, the ill effects of blue sapphire have been noticed. A ring of iron has no side effects.

If the Aggressive Mars or the Plain of Mars is underdeveloped, then a coral can be worn in the ring finger.

The Mount of Sun is normally depressed. If there are vertical lines on the Mount of Sun or if the ring finger is longer than normal, then consider the Mount of Sun as good as developed. If there are horizontal lines on the Mount of Sun or if there is a cross or if the ring finger is smaller than normal, then a ruby worn in the ring finger will prove beneficial.

If the little finger is smaller than normal and this finger is set lower on the palm then an emerald ring should be worn in the little finger. If the Mount of Venus is not well developed then wear a coral in the ring finger.

Phalit jyotish (horoscope reading) advises one to wear a diamond to remove the defects of Venus, but the diamond is a water-dominated stone, while the underdeveloped state of the Mount of Venus conveys that the client lacks in fire. The fire element is connected with sex. This shortcoming is countered by wearing a red gem, i.e. a coral is advisable.

We have suggested the use of these gems on studying the status of various mounts and fingers. If according to the horoscope, there is a defect in some planet, then the advice given by the acknowledged jyotishi (horoscope reader) should be respected.

If the Mount of Moon or Luna Mount is underdeveloped or is defective, then a pearl ring should be worn in the ring finger. If the Defensive Mars is underdeveloped, then an emerald ring is advisable.

The gems should be worn on the hand that is in active use, i.e. the hand with which one writes.

### Weight of Gems for Use on Particular Fingers

A gem weighing 700 to 800 milligrams is ideal. It is feasible to wear a pukhraj or a yellow sapphire in the index finger and an iron ring in the middle finger. To overcome the defects of Mercury, an emerald should be worn in the little finger and to increase the effects of Defensive Mars, the emerald ring should be worn in the ring finger. For wearing ruby, pearl or coral, the ring finger has been earmarked.

### Substitute for Precious Gems

If the person is not in a position to afford a precious gem, then instead of a pearl or emerald, he can wear a silver ring. Similarly in place of a ruby, a coral or yellow sapphire a copper ring will prove beneficial.

To increase the effects of these cheap alternatives, the client should do tratak exercise on the silver or copper ring for 15 to 30 seconds daily. Subsequently, after closing his eyes, he should mediate on his God. This way the effect of this ring equals the impact of the precious gem in the ring. The procedure for tratak has been described earlier in this chapter.

**Suitable Day for Wearing the Ring**

To give strength to the Mount of Sun, the ring should be worn on a Sunday. The ring connected to the Mount of Moon should be worn on a Monday, and rings to be worn for removing the defects of the Mounts of Mars or Mercury or Venus or Saturn should be worn on days related to them.

**Use of Coloured Clothes**

Some of our clients feel discomfort on wearing a ring. For them a suitable alternative would be to wear suitable coloured clothes.

If the Mount of Jupiter is underdeveloped or the index finger is smaller than normal, then clothes of light yellow colour prove a good substitute.

In place of a ring of iron, the client can be advised to wear light blue coloured clothes. A suitable substitute for ruby is pink-coloured clothes; in place of emerald, green clothes can be worn and in place of coral, red clothes are advisable. Instead of wearing a pearl, white clothes can be worn.

In addition to these remedies, it may be remembered that faith in the advice of the palmist plays a prominent role and equally essential are the good wishes of the palmist for his client.

***Books on Palmistry written by Prof. Dayanand/ Nisha Ghai***

- All the Secrets of Palmistry for Profession and Popularity: Rs. 125
- Palmistry: How to Master it: Rs. 125
- A Hand Book of Scientific & Practical Palmistry: Rs. 85
- Palmistry Guide: Rs. 60

***Other Books on Spirituality written by Prof. Dayanand***

- The Bhagvad Gita: A Modern Interpretation: Rs. 295
- Dhyan Yoga: Rs. 60

***The Author***

**Prof. Dayanand** is founder of the Institute of Palmistry and has authored books on palmistry, spiritualism and psychology. He has been practicing palmistry for the past 40 years, while simultaneously conducting research on the subject. Observations and findings on his research coupled with his long experience in the field of palmistry can be seen in his books. Many TV channels telecast his programmes on palmistry.

**Nisha Ghai** is Director, Institute of Palmistry and has written the book entitled *Palmistry Guide.* She has been assisting Prof. Dayanand in reading palms and making predictions for more than a decade. She contributes articles to leading magazines like *Grahlakshmi, Narittva* and to leading newspapers. She has appeared on many TV channels and is an astrologer-advisor for sify.com and indiatimes.com